ANGELA SEITZ

#1 Guide for Men

MY L♥VE LIFE Sucks

The Smart Man's Guide to
UNLOCKING
Your Natural Power of
Charisma and Attracting
Beautiful Women
with Confidence

DEDICATION

To my family whom without their love and support everything else would be meaningless. I would also like to dedicate this book to my mentor and best friend Dave West who is such a positive force in my life.

And finally, to all those who lead monotonous love lives and are ready for a change. I dedicate this book to you for allowing me to share in your journey so that you may experience the butterflies, delicious delights and many adventures of an exciting love life!

CONTENTS

INTRODUCTION

If you always do what you've always done, you'll always get what you've always gotten

- Mark Twain

HEAVEN, EARTH AND dating were all created for men and women to have fun while on this journey called life. That's the honest truth.

Men were not put on this earth to be unhappy with their love lives. I'm sorry to hear that your love life is not as fabulous as you want it to be. I'm going to help you change that. I'm going to help you change that in a big way.

Imagine this: you stroll off a private jet and enter the resort town of Punta Cana. The only thing more beautiful than the blue sky, the white sand beaches that stretch as far as the eye can see, and the crystal-clear waters is the bevy of beauties relaxing along the shore.

These attractive and intelligent women are waiting to meet you!

There's Melissa. She's 5'10, blonde and brilliant. She's got a Law Degree.

There's Claire. She's 5'4. A busty brunette and a bright college student.

There's Emily. She's thin, compassionate and strikingly

attractive. She manages her own online health and fitness business.

There's Mia. She's a stunningly gorgeous native who owns and operates a brick and mortar tourism business.

Your **mission**, should you choose to accept it, is to use your charisma to secure a date with one of these women.

Charisma in this book means: having a proclivity to allure, charm or attract women with whom you want to be romantically involved.

If you can't imagine walking past these women with the confidence that you can date or seduce any one of them, just sit tight, because by the end of this book you'll be able to do just that.

YOUR VISION

Be clear about what you want in your dating life; this knowledge is important. Do you want to 'do you' and figure things out as you go (but not being opposed to settling down if you find the right one)?

Perhaps you can't see yourself settling down anytime soon, so you just want to casually date and have occasional one-night stands? Or, maybe you want a serious long-term relationship with a girlfriend, or a wife?

Dating and wanting to date makes men and woman nervous, and for a good reason. Even if a woman is the most beautiful creature you've ever laid eyes upon, mingling and dating make butterflies dance in their flat tummies.

It's usually a good type of nervousness, like the anxiety one feels when one receives an expensive gift or a digital toy, or when your career moves in a new direction. New things and changes cause men and women alike to experience a nervous excitement.

I have a friend who is a dynamic speaker and who often wows her audiences when she takes the stage. The ends of her speeches are usually met with standing ovations. Yet every time she takes the stage, she feels butterflies in her stomach.

This feeling is exactly what a woman goes through when she is out mingling in the hopes of attracting a man.

She feels a good kind of anxiety because she believes you (yes, you) are fine as hell, and she is worried you won't approach her.

Maybe she's with a group of friends and is apprehensive about you picking one of them over her.

She could be jittery because she has another commitment and must leave soon. She needs you to hurry up and use the 'three-second rule' to establish a connection with her before then.

The three-second rule, for those of you who don't know, is designed to encourage a man to approach a woman fast enough to prevent his internal voice from talking him out of it.

You don't have to count to three and then go, but you do want to approach her in a timely manner if she's checking you out, and *vice versa.*

Those are the best-case scenarios. Now, wait for it…

The worst-case scenario is that she is not nervous in a good way but rather is agitated. Her body language is signaling that she would rather have the world as we know it come to an end than have you in her personal space.

Maybe it's the way your hesitation is turning three seconds into three minutes, and then into thirty minutes.

Maybe it's the way your body language is screaming, *"I'm a total bore!"*

She could be worried that you'll approach her at the same time her jealous boyfriend arrives. She knows he makes too big of a deal when other men express an interest in her, even though they mostly don't mean any harm or even know that she has a boyfriend.

She could be someone who suffers from anxiety attacks and she's trying her best to be calm at a social gathering where lots of nervous energy and excitement are in the atmosphere.

My point is this: she's on edge. If she's someone that you'd like to meet, you've got to use some charm to break the ice, even though you too are nervous. You either talk to her or you go home alone (again).

HOW JACK WON OVER JENNY

A friend of mine, **Jenny** (not her real name) was at a coffee shop reading a book when she took a quick glance at a guy who was checking her out from across the room. From her perspective, he didn't look very interesting, or like a guy she'd go out on a date with. Hoping that this unassuming guy wouldn't invade her personal space, she begins to hyper-focus on her electronic device.

Jack (not his real name) didn't let what he thought was her nervous energy stop him. He approached Jenny, handed her a book on photography and asked if she liked art. Jenny said no and handed the book back, with a look on her face that simply stated, *"I'm not interested."*

Jack graciously takes the book back, but Jack is a fast thinker. Instead of going away, he quickly writes a note and hands the book back to Jenny with the note. She reads the note, which says, *"I can picture you and I together."*

The corniest written pick up line ever, no doubt, but it worked.

It made her smile, which made him smile, and she noticed that he had one of the most gorgeous smiles she'd ever seen. She liked that he had a sense of humor and she found his confidence alluring.

Jack may have looked ordinary, but he was anything but. He had a healthy blend of confidence, humor and quick thinking, all of which won Jenny over.

If Jack had taken the book back and sulked away, that would have been the end of the story. Jack, however, was quick on his feet and quickly tried a different approach on the spot. He, as Jenny would later find out after dating him for a few months, is able to handle any situation with tenacity; a characteristic which she adores.

Charisma is nothing if you lack confidence and the right mindset. Jack saw something in Jenny that piqued his interest, and he wanted to get to know her. He had a positive attitude about Jenny's initial indication of disinterest. He persevered in the face of her outright rejection, and didn't take it personally.

THE SCIENCE OF SEDUCTION AND CHARISMA

There's a science to charisma and it can be summarized in two words: 'think fast' (according to one study, at least). Researchers at the University of Queensland have determined that the ability to think and act quickly is vital to a person's perception of your charisma.

In an interview conducted with Harvard Business Review, one of the researchers, Bill von Hippel, answered the question of how fast. Mr. von Hippel believed that 'fast' is a few hundred milliseconds. Mr. von Hippel added that those with high mental acuity tend to be rated as being more charismatic than average by their friends.

Jack's ability to think quickly won Jenny over. His first approach of handing Jenny the photography book didn't immediately work, but he, using his ingenuity, wrote a note which he delivered to her with a dose of charm. This started their love connection.

Jack had the right state of mind. The key to having charisma is always to believe that you have what it takes to attract women. Guys like Jack are no more or less charismatic than you are. They put their pants on one leg at a time, just like everyone else.

The reason guys like Jack can turn a rejection into a success story is that his state of mind is on point and he can process information and circumstances with haste.

The study conducted by the University of Queensland concluded that those who were able to think fast and give an answer to a question (even if the answer was completely incorrect) were generally perceived as being more charismatic, as opposed to those who were slow to think and act.

Don't misunderstand me; there's much more to that study and to charisma than just thinking fast. I'll be sharing various studies throughout this book, but I want you to bear in mind that no study is perfect.

There are variables at play which can always alter a study's results or their interpretation. You are a smart man and no doubt realize to take research studies with a grain of salt.

ABOUT THIS BOOK

Everything I share with you in this book comes from a place of deep sincerity towards and an utmost concern for your love life (or lack thereof). You may not always like what I have to say, but I will never lie to you. That's a promise.

As a successful matchmaker, charisma and social interaction coach, I create exceptional and unique dates in a tropical corner of the universe.

I've helped hundreds of my clients from all over the world find love and happiness over the years. I've written this book to help men unlock the power of their charisma, so that they can enjoy an exciting and fulfilling dating life.

Please note that you won't always be a winner in love. In any event, sometimes it's not so much about the destination than it is about the journey, which can be quite exciting.

For the remainder of this book, I want you to kick off your shoes, sit back, relax and allow me to be your personal match-maker, charisma and social interaction coach.

The good news is: developing charisma and improving your dating life isn't about making you into someone that you're not. Authenticity is the cornerstone of charisma. I will help you become a better you, not a different you.

YOU NEED A STRATEGY

No strategy will bear fruit without a clear vision. Your vision is what you want. Your strategy is how you'll get it.

You could be the most alluring man on the planet, but it won't mean that you can attract every woman, every time.

Maybe she doesn't have her act together. Maybe yours is the one in need of an adjustment.

Or maybe, it's just not meant to be. You must be at peace with this possibility.

Your strategy should accept the guidance in this book and should be focused on taking actionable steps. Remember: if you take no action, you get no action!

THE PAYOFF

You are a highly intelligent man, I'll make that assumption because you have taken the time to read this book. I want you to read this book in its entirety and let it wash over you like a pleasant splash of a beach wave. Once you are finished, do take the necessary steps shared and enjoy the payoff of an exciting dating life.

I would caution you against reading this book and then putting it away, never to be seen or opened again. If you do what you've always done, you'll get the results you've always gotten. If that's your intended course of action, stop reading right now.

If, on the other hand, you read this book with a 'growth mindset' (a term which I'll explain a little later), the rewards will be incredible.

When you read this book, you'll learn how to:

- Unlock a women's heart and legs quicker then you've ever imagined
- Have an undeniably masculine presence
- Upgrade yourself from an *"Oh, no…"* to a *"Hell yes!"*
- Fake it until you make it with techniques that will have women flocking to you
- Be a better version of yourself while staying true to yourself
- Have your verbal/nonverbal communication skills complement one another to attract the perfect babe
- Utilize techniques so powerful, they're all but guaranteed to captivate the woman of your dreams
- Assess a woman quickly to determine whether she's someone you should sleep with, date, wed or ignore

- Avoid the most common mistakes men make which com-
promise their dating life

Thus far I've given you the MISSION, the VISION, the
STRATEGY. It's time for the PAYOFF.

Here's to your charismatic and dating happiness!

CHAPTER 1

CHARISMA DECODED

Whether you think you can, or you think you can't, you're right

- Henry Ford

THE MOST IMPORTANT thing you need to do when interacting with a woman who you are interested in romantically, and trust me when I tell you this, because this is important. This is the one thing you must remember, if you don't remember anything else in this book.

The thing you must remember is so easy, so simple, so obvious, that I can't believe you don't already know what it is. Can you take a guess? The one thing you must do is, drum roll please; Be cool.

I'm sorry if that's too simple of an answer for your taste, and you wanted a more complicated answer like the Da Vinci code to unlock the secret to charisma and dating. The truth is, becoming someone who is dateable, likable and someone who has an exciting dating life is not complicated.

If you think it's complicated that's because you make it that way.

Those who make it overly complicated flock to the so-called "love gurus" wagging their tail like a dog in heat paying high prices to look ridiculous. I'm sorry honey, but when you flock to a nightspot using the same tired pick-up lines and techniques like everybody else, you look silly. You don't ooze charisma, you ooze ri-DIC-u-lous-ness.

It's ridiculous to spend money and time learning to become someone that you are not. If you are not careful you will become someone that you won't recognize. Think about someone who has gone overboard with plastic surgery, they are unrecognizable.

That's going to be you if you keep taking dating courses and reading books that teach you to think and act like someone else.

The key to being charismatic and having a fun dating life, is to become a better version of you. I'll give you the tools and show you the techniques to do so.

As a matchmaker, charisma and social interaction coach with a degree in psychology, I have a deep understanding of things that unlock the heart, and what makes men and women tick. I love helping my clients find love amidst their busy schedules and in this book, I'm giving you everything I teach to help them have an exciting dating life and achieve relationship goals.

Bringing people together as a successful matchmaker would not be possible if once I connected a man to a woman, he did not have what it takes to keep her interested. I'm going to show you what it takes to be more charismatic and have a really exciting dating life.

If you bungle something, it's OK. Be cool. Trust me, you will recover from any worse case scenario.

The guys who have fun dating and who wreak of charisma do so because they just don't care.

Oh yes, they care about dating and having an exciting love

life, but they get that if they don't get it right each and every time, the world will not end.

There could be any number of issues going on with a woman that has nothing to do with you. Sometimes it's not about you. Her stuff is messed up. Her head is up another's guy's butt.

Don't sweat it. With each new day and new date brings a new opportunity to get it right.

WHAT IS THIS THING CALLED CHARISMA?

The screening process I use to select women from our matchmaking database is often informal and laid back, it feels as if we are a group of friends sharing drinks and laughs. This informal atmosphere tells me a lot about personalities, likes and dislikes.

In this informal setting, I'll often throw out questions to which I want answers. The first question I ask potential ladies is what makes a man charismatic?

Of course, I won't drop real names so I'll use the name of the ladies in the pretend scenario in the opening chapter. Furthermore, these answers have been condensed to reflect the overall answers that I often get.

What is your definition of the word charisma? Give me your honest answer quickly, keeping in mind that there is no right or wrong answer.

Melissa: Someone who has charisma is good looking.

Claire: Those who possess charisma use trickery to get what they want. My older brother is charismatic and always bragging that he uses his charm to manipulate women.

Emily: Men with charisma are easy to talk and connect with. They usually have good personalities.

Mia: The beaches in Punta Cana have charisma.

If a woman can't quite pinpoint charisma's definition, she'll often name a thing or person that reminds her of the word.

Beaches have charisma. So and So has charisma. Remember that I told the ladies there is no right or wrong answer and wanted the first thing that came to them.

Sometimes I'll switch the question up a little and ask women something like: What makes a man charismatic?

As you can imagine I get a variety of answers when women can't pinpoint something specific that turns her on about a man.

I get answers like, "There's something about him that I like/love but I can't explain it exactly." The characteristic that women can't put their finger on, but that some men exude is charisma.

When I ask the men for the purposes of matchmaking, "What makes you charismatic?" Some men freeze.

It's not a trick question and I'm often taken aback that the answer doesn't roll off the tongue. If a man appears lost for words, I'll tighten the question. "Name one thing that makes you charismatic?"

Sometimes I'll offer up a little help. You are powerful. You have a presence. They may offer up that they believe they are a likable guy.

Melissa (from above) states that a person who is attractive is charismatic. However, some women don't associate a man's attractiveness with him being charismatic. What one woman might find appealing another might find appalling.

Case in point, Conor McGregor. I know at least one lady who believes he is a very handsome guy. McGregor is an Irish mixed martial artist who has gained popularity in the US because he has used his skills from the UFC cage in the boxing ring while taking on Floyd Mayweather, a boxer who is widely considered one of the greatest of his era.

I'm not a boxing or MMA aficionado. But as a social interaction coach, I know charisma "swag" when I see it. Keep in mind that McGregor is in an industry where people talk trash and flash cash. His flashy style of charisma – loud, boisterous, concentrated, is not for everyone and certainly not for a few of my reserved clients.

The key point that I will stress throughout this book is to thine own self be true. This means if you are a laid-back kind of guy and see yourself more as a silent type, you don't have to turn your charisma level up to a volume where you are suddenly the life of the party (trash talking loud mouth). Instead, you want to find a middle ground that feels comfortable.

The interesting thing about McGregor, someone who I'll cover in greater detail throughout this book, is that he's great at being present in the moment and can adjust his charisma to any atmosphere. He has what author and researcher Olivia Fox Cabane calls "instant charisma".

Fox Cabane shares that there are three things a person can do to display instant charisma, and McGregor nails it repeatedly in interviews.

Lower your voice tone

Don't be so quick to nod

Pause a couple of seconds before you speak

If he says something outlandish it's because he wants to.

At the other end of the charisma spectrum is TV evangelist Joel Osteen, who speaks with such thoughtful precision that you'd think when he was a child, his mom baked him apple pies daily because his public persona is southern sweet, and thoughtful.

If you ever take a peek at one of Osteen's sermons, you will notice that even when he messes up, which seems like never, he remains calm and confident. Osteen and McGregor appear as different as night and day, yet they both have swag and both are very charismatic.

They both are able, it seems, to adjust to any atmosphere. The thing about being charismatic is that no two charisma types are alike and not everyone finds every attribute in a person charismatic. Both McGregor and Osteen are such powerful charismatic figures that I share more about them in later chapters.

Strong charismatic traits are something every woman wants in a man, and it's an attribute that every man wants to possess. Although there are no right or wrong answers as to the definition of charisma many agree on the attributes associated with the word.

For instance, here's how **Psychology Today** defines charisma.

It is the ability to attract, charm, and influence the people around you. Charisma is often said to be a mysterious ineffable quality - you either have it or don't have it - but it's actually easy to break down many of the key factors that make someone charismatic. Such factors include, but are not limited to: confidence, exuberance, optimism, a ready smile, expressive body language, and a friendly, passionate voice.

I define charisma in this book as having a proclivity to allure, charm or attract women with whom you want to be romantically involved or date.

20th-century German sociologist Max Weber, who is known for his analysis of motives behind human behavior, rebirthed the secular meaning of the word charisma. Weber defined charisma as "a quality that sets an individual apart from ordinary men and causes others to treat him as endowed with supernatural, superhuman, or at least exceptional powers or qualities."

He also stated, "such qualities are not accessible to the ordinary person". But what does Weber know, he married his second cousin.

Since Weber reintroduced the word charisma and its meaning in the 20th century, it seems that definition was birthed into the subconscious of fools who believe that only people born with charisma can have it and that it's an "innate quality".

Richard Wiseman, a lead researcher in charisma, estimated that it is 50% innate and 50% learned. This means if you don't naturally have it you can still bolster your charisma and improve your dating appeal.

If you look at McGregor's early interviews or Osteen's earlier sermons, they always appeared likable but they didn't ooze charisma like they do now. This supports the claim that 50% is innate and 50% is learned. Smart men like you in the 21st century know that anything you are willing to practice and take the time to learn, can be learned, including charisma.

Definitions of charisma differ slightly, although there are core attributes that people with charisma have and traits they exude. As I share what they are, I want you to remember the only thing you need to remember if you mess up is, it's OK.

WHAT THEY HAVE THAT YOU DON'T

Indeed, it seems that some people are born with charisma. They have an irresistible personal magnetism that women flock to. They appear to be so irresistible that a woman like Melissa can't explain the attraction. *"It's just something about him that I like but can't pinpoint."*

Osteen and McGregor put their pants on one leg at a time like you. Prayer is not what makes Televangelist Osteen have "it". Punching is not what makes McGregor have "it." They don't have any special power. Remember, Charisma is part innate and partly learned.

Their secret if there is one, is that they don't walk around over-thinking what they do and say. They don't wear fear on their sleeve like a badge.

Fear is a punch in the gut. According to Nathan DeWall a professor of psychology at the University of Kentucky, the fear of being rejected can feel like someone has punched you in the stomach. Ouch.

Researchers at the University of Michigan found that the consequences of social rejection can feel similar to being physically hurt.

Fear begets more fear of being rejected, and then becomes a self-fulfilling prophecy of you believing it and therefore your belief becomes truth. You believe a woman is going to reject you and your body sets off un-charismatic biological reactions of rejections, and she rejects you.

Fear is painful and ego is the enemy. A man's ego can sometimes keep them from trying to improve and or being present in the moment. Your ego operates very much like your inner critic. What your inner critic taketh away, your ego giveth.

The inner critic tells you, "you are not shit." The ego tells you "you are the shit". Your ego tells you all that you really have to do is be cool and relax, because if you make a mistake it's not the end of the world. Your inner critic tells you, you can do no right.

You are confused. Don't be, as I stated earlier the one thing you have to do, along with other self-improvement stuff, is be cool.

You might not get everything right overnight, but reading this book is another step in becoming more charismatic and improving your dating life.

A BETTER YOU

One of my favorite quotes is perched at the top of this chapter. It's about the power of belief and having the right mindset. I firmly believe that whether you think you can, or you think you can't, you're right.

Words are very important. If you think you can have charisma and a better more fun dating life you can. Mindset is very important. Renowned psychologist Carol Dweck pioneered the concept of fixed vs. growth mindset.

When a man has a fixed mindset towards improving his dating life he'll think negatively and have a negative outlook on his dating life. When he goes out mingling he'll mind-whine (whining to yourself) that it's a waste of time to go out and that he probably won't meet anyone.

He might tell himself something like, "I'm just not the type of guy that women are attracted too, not attractive women anyway." Or if you according to you, somehow managed to get a date you might believe, "I won't ever be able to keep her interested in me on a date." This is the work of your inner critic and a fixed mindset.

Or maybe your ego-driven fixed mindset is telling you the reason you don't date more is that too many women have issues. The ego says "Too many women have issues which is why I'll never get a date."

Not only does a fixed mindset mess up your short-term outlook, but it also prevents your ability to grow and learn how to be more charismatic and get more dates.

With a fixed mindset you might eventually stop going out altogether because after all, what's the point? The point is whether you think it will work out or whether you think it won't, you are correct. Don't shoot yourself in the foot before you take the first step.

Meanwhile, a man with a growth mindset believes anyone can improve their dating life or become more charismatic. This man knows that whether he thinks he can or thinks he can't, he's correct. He knows that a better dating life or becoming more charismatic is entirely due to the actions he takes.

With a growth mindset a man thinks, "Any man can have an exciting dating life and become more charismatic. It's not totally innate."

DATING DECODED

Needing validation is another thing that could be making your dating life more complicated then it has to be.

I have a girlfriend who was dating a guy who was always saying what she considered to be ridiculous things. One time she shared that he told her he needs a woman to call him in the middle of the day and tell him what exciting adventure she had planned for him.

What he needs goes beyond a call, he needs validation. He was depending on her to make his life better and that was a big mistake.

Therein lies the problem in that you have probably worked hard (taken action) so that you aren't a hot mess and so now you need some type of validation.

You need someone to make you feel good. However, feeling good starts with you.

Men run into trouble when they focus on outward aspects of improving dating life and not the inward stuff. When you focus on the outward dating stuff you crave rewards.

Maybe you've overcome a lot to get to the point where you are now dateable. You've taken action and you should be proud.

Maybe you've spent months working on improving you which is great (you've taken action) and was necessary (since you were a hot mess) and since before this you haven't been successful at dating. When you did land a date, you couldn't land the second one.

Now that you've gone through the efforts with your GROWTH MINDSET to improve yourself and have gone through a transformation you want accolades and approval.

Look at me I'm better than before. Tell me that I'm better or that I'm good. You need affirmation that you have made self-improvement.

I'm sorry my dear needy man, a woman just meeting you or who is just getting to know you doesn't know and frankly she doesn't care how far you've come. You've come a long way baby but so what.

She doesn't know your backstory and she may never need to know it, not at this stage of the dating game anyway.

If you need a pat on the back, do it yourself.

If you need validation, do it yourself because how you feel first and foremost should come from the inside. If you need a woman to constantly shower you with praises of how wonderful and charming you are, how good you treat her, your dating life is going to be in trouble from the outset.

Don't hold your breath waiting for someone else who really knows very little about you to shower you with outward validations. Instead of waiting for a Scooby snack because of your life improvements, just be that better person and keep pressing forward, and continue to grow.

Stop believing you can only feel good through a woman's validation. Stop comparing yourself to someone who you are not. I know that advice might be a little hard. It's human nature to look at someone and see how you stack up against them.

All men (and women) do it. But think of it like this, it's your race to win. Maybe you can't be a man who appears to have it all, although you can strive to be a better version of yourself and carve out your own exciting dating life and charismatic style.

Charisma decoded is also having emotional intelligence. Emotional intelligence is a set of words that I constantly share.

Emotional intelligence can be looked at as having common sense. This is essentially understanding the social dynamics of the atmosphere.

When Conor McGregor is trying to sell tickets to his fight he's a loud trash talking fighter.

When he is interviewing in his neighborhood, talking about overcoming adversities or helping kids, he strikes a different tone and that's using emotional intelligence.

Televangelist Osteen epitomizes emotional intelligence with the sermons he delivers.

Let's pretend that he had a sermon prepared that he's been working on for weeks and the week he prepares to deliver that sermon something happens that makes his sermon not right at the particular time. Osteen wouldn't use the sermon.

Charisma and dating aren't as complicated as unlocking a bitcoin, that's a complicated mathematical formula. Every charismatic man I know, or have studied, is an all-around relaxed person and this includes when they are in social settings.

They always have the right vibe. If they misstep, they don't make a big deal out of it. Even if they feel a sense of discomfort they work through it.

What you must remember is that a misstep or a misspeak is not a big deal. A fuck-up is like a wave on the beach. It will get you wet, it might make you fall down, but nine times out of ten it won't destroy you. It happens and then it's over with. If you mess up, it's not the end of the world, and so what, just be cool.

KEY TAKEAWAYS

Charisma decoded can be summed up in two words *Be Cool*. You are going to make mistakes in this thing called dating and it's OK. It's not dating mistakes that matter, but how you recover.

Women have different definitions of the word charisma. Don't try to be like everybody else. Instead strive to be a better version of yourself.

MMA fighter Conor McGregor and Televangelist Joel Osteen have different styles of charisma. Their secret to oozing charisma is that they don't walk around overthinking what they do and say. They don't wear fear on their sleeve like a badge.

According to research the fear of being rejected can feel like someone has physically hurt you.

Researcher Fox Cabane sums up charisma like this: Lower your voice tone. Don't be quick to nod. Pause before you speak.

Psychology Today defines charisma as the ability to attract, charm and influence people around you.

Charisma is not a mysterious ineffable quality.

Having charisma means you have a proclivity to allure, charm or attract women with whom you want to be romantically involved.

20th-century German sociologist Max Weber, rebirthed the secular meaning of the word charisma and possibly because of him some see it as an ineffable quality, not easy to obtain.

Researcher Wiseman concludes 50% of charisma is innate and 50% is learned. Smart people like you reading this book know that you can improve your authentic self and be more charismatic. This means if you don't have it you can practice and get it.

While definitions of charisma differ slightly, there are core attributes that people with charisma have and traits they exude. The important thing to remember is if you mess, it's OK.

The best quote ever is one attributed to American business-man and automaker Henry Ford. Ford said, "Whether you think you can, or you think you can't, you're right." If you think you can have charisma and a better more fun dating life you can.

Focus on the inward growth of being a better you. Don't expect women you meet to give you validation.

Having a Growth mindset is very important. So is having emotional intelligence.

To be present, you must first have the right mindset. Renowned psychologist Carol Dweck has pioneered the concept of fixed vs. growth mindset. If your mind is fixed there's no room for improvement.

CHAPTER 2

AUTHENTIC CHARISMA

The privilege of a lifetime is to become who you truly are

– C.G. Jung

AT THE HEART of charisma and dating is authenticity. In this chapter you'll discover how to bring out the best of who you are.

I'm willing to bet that most of the dating advice you've received so far is keeping you single (or alone), especially if it came from a dating course or a "love guru" who specializes in teaching you to act and think like other men.

As a woman I can't teach you to act and think like other men, and even if I could, I wouldn't, because teaching you to act and think like someone you are not is a sure-fire way to keep you dateless.

I don't want to teach you how to be a robot; instead, allow me to share with you ways to become a better version of yourself and enjoy an exciting dating life.

None of the advice I share will do you a jack-bit of good if your actions don't stem from your authentic self. This is your original self before you were influenced by family, friends, and society, and not necessarily in that order.

You don't want to change who you are and become someone you are not; instead, you want to build upon the things that are naturally you and make you likable.

Those are the strengths I will help you tap into which increase your charisma, increase your attractiveness and likeability, and allow you to enjoy a great dating life.

Even if you think you are just an average guy, knowing how to tap into your innate charisma gives you what you need to persuade and excite people, to persuade and excite a woman to date you, hook up with you or to do anything you want. Have you ever been envious of a guy because he has the perfect girlfriend or wife? She is extremely attractive on the inside and out, and treats him like a king.

You wonder how in the hell has this average guy landed the lady with the superstar good looks who is at his beck and call. We are not talking in a domineering way here, but in a genuine way in which she's naturally happy to please him.

The secret is that he exudes the kind of charisma she adores and that excites her. Women are always on the lookout for a man who will bring some excitement into their lives.

To you he might appear average and average looking, but he's got the kind of charisma traits that ups his perceived attractiveness.

Interestingly, it doesn't work the other way around. This means there are a lot of extremely handsome men with lackluster person- alities and if they have a partner, she's not treating him like a king.

You see, even if you are extremely good looking but don't pos- sess charismatic traits – it can actually detract from your appeal.

Throughout this book I'll continuously reference two men

who embody the very definition of authentic charisma. However, these two men are as opposite as day and night.

One of them has been called the most charismatic man on earth and the other brags about ripping off heads. These two people are televangelist Joel Osteen and MMA fighter Conor McGregor, who I'll cover later in this chapter.

Osteen's and McGregor's public personalities are nothing alike, yet they ooze charisma and have millions of followers and fans from around the world.

Before we move on, let me be clear. It doesn't matter if you are religious or nonreligious, whether you are into sports or not into sports, or whether you hate Osteen's or McGregor's guts. All that matters - the only lesson I want you to take from this is that both men are intensely charismatic despite their vastly different public personas.

This is an important point to make because learning to be more charismatic and enjoying a better dating life is not just about teaching you to be like someone you are not, because the problem is that if those behaviors are not in sync with the essence of who you truly are inside, you come across as fake. When I use the phrase in parts of this book "Fake it until you make it", it's not to turn you into someone you are not or worse, block your innate charisma.

Nor is teaching you to be more charismatic and having a better dating life just about teaching you to "just be yourself." Because if just being yourself isn't cutting it, then you want to make improvements. To see why teaching you to be like someone else or to "just be yourself" isn't the answer, let's take a look at Osteen's story.

When televangelist Joel Osteen took over at his father's church he tried to copy his father's style of preaching which was called fire and brimstone, a style of preaching that threatens punishment in the hereafter unless you do what the Bible says.

However, Osteen quickly discovered that style of preaching did not feel authentic for him. He worried that unless he preached the way his father did, the five-thousand-member church would lose members. Yet instead of copying his father's style, he decided to go with a style of preaching that felt authentically like himself.

His style of preaching was laid back, light-hearted and tinged with humor. Do you think the churchgoers rejected him? Absolutely not - the church went from 5,000 to 25,000 members.

Why do you think the church grew in numbers instead of decreasing when Osteen took over? It's for a couple of reasons.

One reason is that humans like variety. If you like apple pie it doesn't mean you can't also like key lime pie. If you prefer blondes it doesn't mean that you don't like brunettes too. You can like both or a variety, even though you might like one more than the other.

You might think the advice that was better suited for Osteen was to "just be himself", advice he was given. However, Osteen readily admits that the advice "just be yourself" was not going to cut it if he wished to go from a preacher's kid, who started out afraid to speak in public, to one of the most charismatic speakers in the world.

In a 2014 interview, Osteen stated that he writes out his 28-minute message word for word and then spends about six hours reviewing it. He says he delivers his speech twice before the third sermon, which is televised.

The moral of the Osteen story is to thine own self be true, but practice, practice, practice for a better you.

In the *Decoded Chapter* I share that there is no right or wrong answer for someone's perceived definition of charisma. You'll recall that one woman who I asked what her definition of charisma was, stated that charisma is all about manipulation.

She learned from her brother that someone who is charismatic manipulates people to get what they want. Because of what she was taught, she saw charisma and persuasion as bad. Her definition is her opinion, neither wrong or right.

There are people who persuade others in an attempt to manipulate them. But there are also people that persuade people in what they claim is a good way. Again, it doesn't matter if you agree, disagree or hate Osteen. He presents that he persuades followers in a way that he believes is good.

McGregor persuades people to root for him in the cage or ring. Just like there are many ways to persuade people, there are many styles of charisma and you might only like one style or many, or prefer one style over the other.

THE FEAR OF THE AUTHENTIC SELF

The challenge with men who hide who they really are or try to be someone they are not is that they try to fit in, and society has conditioned them that they can only fit in if they are a certain way.

Think about when you were growing up; who were the cool kids? The cool kids were attractive, sports stars and cheerleaders, outgoing, fun and the life of the party.

On the other hand, the kids who were geeky, nerdy, quiet, and unassuming were viewed as less popular. They may have even been picked on, and so as not to fall into the unpopular group they may have conformed.

Of course, this is a generalization (popular vs. nerdy kids), but the point is that anytime you try to be someone that you are not, you'll quickly discover it's exhausting and often has a negative reaction.

That is to say you have tried to avoid being who you really are because you fear being ridiculed, and that's usually exactly what ends up happening (you get ridiculed), because when you yield to another's expectation and to thine own self you are not true, you come off as a shady replica and people will be turned off by your inauthenticity. Women, just like men, are turned off by fakeness.

The worst thing about being inauthentic is that it strips you of your innate charisma, since experts say at least 50% of charisma is innate; not what was previously thought, which was that you have to be born with it. Be who you are, but also don't oppose self-improvement.

FEAR OF VULNERABILITY

Now you know trying to be someone you are not, like the life of the party, isn't going to work. Instead, you have to open yourself up and be vulnerable. I know men hate vulnerability because the societal message is loud and clear: vulnerability in men is a sign of weakness.

It gets confusing because for your entire life you've been advised not to show emotion while also being told to be real. Let me show you how this plays out.

There's this pop singer/actor. He's very attractive. Or was. He became popular because of landing a singing jingle for a beverage company and then later doing these guy-oriented action movies that broke movie blockbuster numbers.

The more popular he became, the more arrogant he grew. It's reported that he has repeatedly said disparaging things about women. As is the case with the digital disruption era, social media went nuts and ripped him a new one. Some men sided with him "You the Man" and women, uh, not so much.

The higher his star profile rose, the deeper he floated into arrogance territory and his ego got the best of him, it seems. So, it probably comes as no surprise that a few years later, when the guy put out a video on social media with him having what looked like a melt-down on camera over his impending divorce and the large amount of alimony and child support he was being ordered to pay, and to top that off he was being denied joint custody of his child because of physical abuse allegations, he received little sympathy.

Because of his past public displays of arrogance, let's just say the social media-ites weren't too kind. Some ripped him a new one. One comment read, "Why is he sobbing? He looks so ugly?" Another comment said, "If he has to cry, why do it in public?"

There is no way for me to know, but it's not unreasonable to guess that the reason this celebrity for many years put on this big macho façade or was really arrogant is because he feared being vulnerable as a sign of weakness. Men don't like to show flaws or vulnerability for fear it will be viewed unfavorably.

Flaws equal rejection, and rejection equals a punch in the gut. It seems this singer/actor was willing to do anything to avoid an "ego death".

"Ego death" (a term I'll also discuss in greater detail later) is the fear of humiliation, shame or any other mechanism of profound self-disapproval that threatens the loss of integrity of the self.

It is the fear of shattering or disintegrating one's constructed sense of lovability, capability, and worthiness, according to an article that appears in *Psychology Today*.

The pop singer/actor's ego might scream "How could any woman resist you? You are famous, rich, good looking, and talented! You can say whatever you want about women."

The inner critic might whisper, "These beautiful women are only throwing themselves at you because you are famous and have money." This is when ego jumps back in, "You can do no wrong."

The pop singer takes the side of ego, to avoid ego death. He speaks rudely, always two steps behind common sense that he can say whatever he wants with no consequences.

I don't believe that if this celebrity had been a bit more popular with women he would have received this type of backlash, but even if so, know that there are always going to be what I call "haters" and "congratulators".

Both celebrities and average Joes have them. I know a guy, an average Joe, who, when he broke up with his girlfriend, out of the woodwork came the "haters" and those he shared with the "congratulators".

The haters found out about his breakup at their own pity party. The reflection of how they criticized him is a reflection of how they treat themselves: badly. They have a lot of issues and they are happy to add new members to their unhappy club.

On the other hand, are the "congratulators" (not meaning those who congratulate you on your breakup, but instead those he shared with and who have compassion and didn't see his relationship breakup as him failing). These are the mature people and also the people who really care about him and show compassion and understanding.

Think about a person you truly love and care about, whether it's a good friend, a relative or your partner. You would never tear them down by making them feel weak and shameful.

If you feel vulnerable it might help you to remember that there are 7 billion people on this earth and probably half of them are men, and likely half of them feel or have felt vulnerable. I can say this with certainty because in life you are going to always find yourself in vulnerable situations.

You could lose your job or company. You could become sick and gain or lose a lot of weight. You could have problems with sexual dysfunction; whatever the case, you can't avoid vulnerable situations.

Vulnerability runs the gamut of everyday people and celebrities who don't feel wealthy enough, handsome enough, strong enough. These feelings trigger shame and that's because vulnerability is a powerful emotion that brings about heartache, heartbreak, pain and disappointment.

To never feel vulnerable is not normal. It's not human because all humans are flawed and it's the flaw, the imperfection that gets to the heart of what makes you authentic.

Vulnerability is not weak or submissiveness; on the contrary it is the courage to be yourself, to be courageous, to be authentic.

CONOR MCGREGOR IS THE "V" WORD

When I started the research for this book I went back and looked at some earlier McGregor interviews in which he openly admitted to working crappy jobs and being on social assistance, the welfare program in Ireland.

He shared that receiving public assistance and not earning enough to care for himself did not make him feel good. In sharing his hardships, he showed vulnerability.

Part of feeling manly and strong is being able to take care of yourself and those you love, and that's not the way McGregor felt when he was getting help.

McGregor got it right when he comforted his vulnerable

feelings, which allowed him to push past fear and rise above his poverty. He embraced the benefits of being vulnerable.

The Benefits:

Embracing vulnerability allows you to be challenged and grow. If life was just easy breezy you might not feel the need to reach your full potential. For example, if McGregor had not felt the sting of poverty he might not have challenged himself to become the big success he is.

If Osteen was naturally a good public speaker he might not have challenged himself to become a great speaker.

Embracing vulnerability helps you have more fulfilling and intimate relationships. When you can trust someone, and open up to them, not only will the trusting person, "this congratulator", help you through trying times, but you'll find that connecting with people helps you build better bonds.

Embracing vulnerability allows you to be open and honest, and this will also help you build better bonds as people will see you as trustworthy, a strong trait of charisma. When you don't embrace reality, or face the truth you risk living in shame and secrecy.

Suppose McGregor had tried to hide his past of being on assistance and then became this big celebrity. Do you think his "haters" would have kept quiet?

Embracing vulnerability promotes well-being. When you keep stuff inside because of shame or fear it eats away at you. Osteen was open about the fact that he didn't feel adequate to fill his father shoes. In expressing his concerns I'm sure he received words of encouragement.

MCGREGOR IS THE "A" WORD

McGregor appears to be an authentic celebrity. It might not always seem that way because he's in a sports field where people flash cash and talk trash. To people not familiar with the sport, or those who don't feel that you need to talk trash to succeed in the sport, they might not buy his quieter less flamboyant moments and see him as a flake.

For instance, when McGregor is trying to sell tickets to an upcoming fight, he talks a lot of trash. He's famous for saying he's going to rip someone's head off and hurling insults. This infamous pre-interview act of his probably leads some to believe he's an a-hole.

But when McGregor isn't promoting his upcoming fight, like when he's just doing regular interviews and training, he comes across as a genuinely nice guy. He also comes across this way after a fight, because whether win or lose - and I've watched his interviews after he's gotten his ass kicked, he appears to be quite the gentleman, a far cry from the savage of a man who is hyping fights.

Even though I'm not a fight aficionado, if you research how this market sells tickets then you will get McGregor. If not then you will not.

Another thing that adds to McGregor appearing authentic is that when he interviews and he's not hyping a fight he appears present in the moment, a key trait of authentic charisma. It's not uncommon for McGregor to wear sunglasses in interviews and even though you can't see his eyes, his composure, his upright body language and answers that appear to be well thought out, meaning he listens carefully before he speaks, make him appear authentic and present in the moment.

I'm not sure why he wears the sunglasses; maybe it's part of his brand or maybe his face is beaten up from practice, who knows.

However, it does not take away from his presence, and that's not the case with everyone. I've seen celebrities do interviews with sunglasses and it appears they are high on drugs or hiding something.

And who hasn't seen plenty of interviews with celebrities who don't come across as decent people? It's like they don't want to do the interview or worse, appear arrogant and rude.

It's as if the interviewer and the fans should be grateful regardless of whether they come across as arrogant or full of themselves, as if they are not present in the moment and/or they are above the interviewer or their fans.

Of course, every celebrity and person has an off day, and a celebrity will almost certainly have an "off" interview.

But if you are known for being distracted or defensive in interviews, if you don't want to be there, the arrogance will show on your face and your fans will know it. Arrogance is an easy feature to spot.

A study by James Gross reveals that we connect too deeply as humans for someone to try to pull the wool over our eyes and we (the person who they are being inauthentic to) react physiologically, which makes us feel uncomfortable around fake people. That's why we like authentic people and celebrities.

There is no way to build loyal fans who will pay money to see you if you come across as disrespectful and fake. People perceived as not being genuine appear flakey. Call McGregor a lot of things, but don't call him inauthentic.

If you want to come across as authentic whether you are in a media interview, a job interview or on a DATE, you want to be present in the moment.

I share throughout this book how to be present in the moment and neutralize mental discomfort.

People are human and thus easily distracted, so if you feel yourself getting distracted you might try an exercise like wiggling your toes and concentrating on feeling the sensations to get back on track. Come back to the present moment.

We feel a connection with down-to-earth people who are just who they are.

As you become increasingly comfortable being your authentic self you'll notice that women will naturally be attracted to you. I've never met a man that didn't have a lot of likable traits and I'll go out on a limb and say this includes you too.

KEY TAKEAWAYS

All actions must stem from your authentic self. Love Gurus and dating schools don't teach from a place of authenticity. They teach you to think and act like everybody else.

Build upon the natural things that make you likable. I've never met a man that didn't have several if not many likable traits. Learn how to tap into your innate charisma giving focus to what energizes and excites. List what your likable traits are.

Some women treat their men like Kings and that's because he excites her.

People like Conor and Joel are as different as night and day yet they are both likable and charismatic.

The part of charisma that is not innate takes practice, how much depends on how good you are. Joel Osteen used to handwrite out his sermons and practice it three times.

You don't want to persuade women in an attempt to manipulate them as it will backfire.

We have a vision of cool kids planted in our mind that we need to get over.

It's hard for men to open themselves up and be vulnerable. We say open up, but we laugh and ridicule men if they do.

Fear is so powerful that it feels like you've been punched in the gut and a man will do anything to avoid ego death. The inner critic and ego will battle for your soul.

Simply put, you are going to have haters and congratulators. Haters are going to hate. Congratulators will show empathy.

CHAPTER 3

CHARISMA'S POWER TRAITS

The starting point of all achievement is desire

\- Napoleon Hill

YOU ALREADY KNOW or can take an educated guess as to what quality gives men a football-field-wide advantage in finding romance and dating women. Hint - it's in the book's title, it's in the chapter's title, it's "charisma".

Having charisma gives you a top advantage and makes you more likable, dateable, fuckable, but not necessarily in that order.

The more of a "success object" you are, the more charismatic you will appear, and the more women will be naturally attracted to you.

We are an instantaneously driven society, meaning we want what we want fairly quickly. We want someone who on day one comes out of a well-put-together package.

If I could wave a magic wand and present before you a room full of hot babes who possess the specific qualities you're looking for in an ideal woman, you'd like that, wouldn't you?

While I don't wave wands, I do have stellar matchmaking

skills, but even as a skilled matchmaker, it's still up to you to do your part in the charm department to unlock her legs or heart, or whatever it is you want.

Some are born with it, some work for it, some work like hell to get it, and some fake it until they make it. That is to say, they already have or they project many of the ingredients of charisma to have a more exciting dating life.

If you want to start off with a charismatic advantage, then you'll quite naturally be at an advantage if you have the things on the **POWER** list below to pair with other charisma attributes.

I present to you the power list, and I want you to read it carefully. Not because you are living on Mars and don't know or can't guess what things attract women, but read the list as a refresher as you go down this new charismatic path.

Sometimes guys who think they know everything don't know as much as they think. After the power list of charismatic attributes, I will reveal the secondary list of things you can do to fake it until you make it.

I want to be clear here - I don't use the phrase "Fake it until you Make it" in the sense that you should be inauthentic, because to rev up your dating life you have to come from an authentic place, and authenticity is the heart of this book.

If it is inauthentic you can still get the same results, although they won't last and drama will surely follow, as you'll see in the examples I share.

MONEY. SURPRISE! Money makes you feel confident and secure, which exudes charisma and makes you a good catch. You don't have to be a part of the billionaire's club, although it certainly couldn't hurt.

It also wouldn't hurt if you have more than enough money to pay your bills and to play around with. You are not going to feel confident if you have money issues, if you are losing your house, car, or living in your parent's basement. If you want to exude charisma then improve your financial situation.

A male friend asked me, as if he genuinely didn't know, "Why does money turn women on so much? I don't get it, since money is not connected to love or affection." He went on to say, "Money cannot love you, cannot keep you warm in bed at night, cannot protect you from danger, cannot start a family with you, cannot raise your children." This friend was sincerely baffled and continued, saying, "Why does green paper turn women on so much?"

Here's the kicker. My friend went on and on about men being criticized for looking at and wanting women with big breasts and nice asses. He said being attracted to those things is more acceptable since it's how nature programmed men to be.

He went on to say that money is not a natural object and something created to "keep the world going around."

Men, I'm not making this up. Now, granted my friend's beliefs might be a little bit out there, but I do occasionally encounter men who whine that women only want them for their money.

Now don't take this the wrong way honey, but if you are one of the "whiners" then you probably don't have any money. Yes, there are gold diggers, but there are also looks diggers - you like her because she looks attractive. She likes you because you have money.

She is willing to ignore the stuff she does not like about you and vice versa because each of you possesses the most important quality that you are attracted to. Every case, however, is not the "gold digger" or "looks digger" scenario.

The truth is, whether it's a smart and classy woman from good stock, or a dirt-poor woman, a woman who fits somewhere in between, or a quality woman who is a good catch - these types of women have been taught to accept nothing less than the best.

These women will quite naturally be attracted to a man who is financially secure. But even if you have money but don't have any other attributes you won't hold a woman of high quality - you won't hold her interest. To keep her you've got to have some other qualities.

A study in the late 80's on "Human Sexual Selection" by psychologist David Buss and Michael Barnes asked people to rank 76 characteristics as it pertained to what they value most in a potential mate. The results of this study might surprise you in that neither beauty nor wealth topped the list of men and women.

Here are the top three on the list:

1. Kind and understanding
2. Exciting personality
3. Intelligence

Men did value women's appearance more highly than women, and women valued a man's earning potential higher than a man. But as you can see, neither men or women put attractiveness or wealth among their top considerations in that particular study.

However, surprise surprise, in a lot of studies men do put looks first, just as women put money.

A study published by a team of researchers from UCLA and other top universities asked its more than 27,000 participants to rate the importance of different characteristics in long-term partners. The study found that 69% of women prefer men with a steady income and who makes or will make a lot of money.

A frequent conversation I have with women for matchmaking purposes is about financial stability in a man and how they value it. They all prefer a partner who is financially secure. If you meet a woman who doesn't want a good future and safe relationship then run to the hills because she's insane.

If she comes from good stock she can't step down, and if she comes from nothing she doesn't want to relive the insecurities and challenges her family faced in her childhood.

Money - and listen to this loud and clear - is the most powerful resource a man can have.

You having money says to a woman that together you can have an exciting dating life. That if your dating life turns into marriage and babies the family will be secure.

If you don't have a lot of money or no money then you need to be the most ambitious man she's ever met. Ambition is money's stepbrother. Women love ambitious men because she knows even if right now your home is a man cave in your parent's basement, it's only because you are building another digital disrupter for financial freedom.

In this digital age where stuff is just begging to be invented, where you can take online classes to brush up on your skills and increase your wealth, there is no reason for anyone not to be able to improve their finances. Especially if you chase money harder than you chase tail.

If you are not of the generation where you get the concept of making money online, then you might be from the generation where men worked their butts off and there were not a lot of distractions like there are nowadays. This was when the man's man worked long hours, two or three jobs, and was still able to spend quality time with the family. If you are of that generation then you should easily have a hundred grand under your mattress and even more in your savings account.

I'm being a little facetious of course, but the point I'm making is this: not every man has money, but any man can have ambition.

Ambition is the drive to want to do better. You don't have ambition and want to know where to start? Start by reading books to inspire you.

This brings me to another point: a man should be well-read. Reading books can teach you how to make money, shows that you are ambitious and it will help you achieve goals… just wait until you finish this book.

POWER. Power is associated with words like "independence" and "status" and "confident". Powerful men radiate power. The powerful radiations spring from the way they carry themselves, the way they dress, their body movements.

I know a thirty-something young startup guy who was a geek in high school. I saw some of his pictures on social media growing up and he looked like a geek. He's a small guy, but that's not what made him look like an unforgettable pipsqueak.

Instead it was the way he stood in pictures. He may not have been as big as the jocks who stood beside him, but he should not have stood beside them as their personal jockstrap dressed in a funny colored sweatshirt and what we now call mom jeans.

I've seen small guys in pictures with big guys and I can't take my eyes off of them because they stand straight, take up space and show their crotch. Your size isn't an indication of manliness or your worth.

Cut to modern day and this guy looks like he was created from a king's cloth. He's a little bigger now, but it's not his size, it's his presence. He doesn't have an ego, although he could; he could be the revenge of the nerds. He clocks about a quarter of a million dollars per month.

He sent me a link to a video blog of him in Europe when he was there to speak. In the video, he gets out of bed and goes to the sink and brushes his teeth, and the video cuts to him getting dressed. Everything he puts on fits him like a glove, even his hipster socks. When he's completely dressed he looks immaculate. He strikes a pose and you just know he's going to kill it on stage.

Next in the video we see him at a social gathering among a bunch of rich start-up guys with new money. He stands out because he's the best dressed and because of the way he carries himself. He's not a pipsqueak anymore. He's rich, handsome, confident, and he's got a presence.

Presence is another word you'll read a lot in this book because it's so key to the essence of charisma. What does this have to do with you? If you don't already have it, fake it until you make it! If you are among the powerless men there are behaviors you can do to emulate power.

Let's pretend you are the valet guy parking the car. When you take the keys to park the car, be confident, be the best valet in the world. Pretend in your mind if you have to that you are the hotel owner's son, or that in a few weeks you graduate with a Master's degree and already have exciting career options and offers.

Stand next to the Bentley for a moment like you own it. Stand up straight and arch your back, take up a lot of space, more space than the guy who owns the car. Let your crotch area be in full exposure. Let your body language say that you are the man.

Be forewarned that the exposing of crotch stance isn't for everyone, and it goes without saying you should be fully clothed unless you are in an intimate setting with your babe, but if that were the case you wouldn't be reading this book. When you stand or sit fully clothed with your crotch exposed it means you are putting your masculinity on display for the women you would like to attract or for men you are competing against.

This position isn't about sexuality per se as much as it's about masculinity. When you take the standing position, legs spread apart or if sitting legs open, the focus isn't to make yourself look like you have a big male part to attract or offend anyone, instead it's more of a way of saying you are strong and confident.

Countless research studies support that male attractiveness can be manipulated by perceived status and in some cases just doing simple things like standing by an expensive house or car. In a study that appeared in *Pubmed.gov (ncbi.nlm.nih.gov)*, a male model stood beside a Ford Fiesta ST. Next, he stood by a Bentley and was instructed to do the same body posture and the exact facial expression.

Female participants in the study rated the male significantly more attractive just by standing next to the more expensive Bentley car.

Other studies have shown that the opposite is true too. A man who was rich and had a high status did not project confidence regardless of the type of car he drove or what house he lived in, thus women didn't perceive him as attractive.

Maybe you can't rush out and get a $200K Bentley. Maybe the only way you'll get near a Bentley soon is when you park it in your position as a valet at the hotel. But if you have enough ambition and you project power, you will attract high-quality women.

LOOKS. You look how you look. You may never look anything but average or below average, but you can look better. The women I chat with, of all the things that matter to them, looks aren't as important as other qualities.

He was once handsome, and now he's handsomely stitched up. Actors and celebrities do whatever they can to maintain their looks.

You should always strive to look your best, and don't be what I call "looking better adverse." Plastic surgery, hair plugs, weight loss - go for it. Have great hygiene. You don't have to look the best, but you want to look and smell your best.

How good you look is tied to how confident you feel. Do whatever it takes to look better. I find that showering and staying well-groomed is something that sometimes can stump an older man who is a senior. Let's start with our seasoned men who may find themselves back in the dating pool and it's been a minute and they need help in the fashion department. Maybe he is recently widowed and has old money.

In his past relationship, settling into old age and letting it all hang out might have been OK. You get older, you get a little more wrinkled, a little more belly fat, more stains on your teeth. However, many things that eat away at your looks can be fixed.

You may be comfortable with the clothes you have, mothballs and all, and may not care much for this new stuff. Being more well-groomed and styled isn't necessarily about getting caught up in trends because they come and go, but instead having a wardrobe that speaks to the modern man, regardless of your age, is important.

This is a biggie for an older gent - trim your nose hair and ear hair, and be well groomed, even if you are up in age. I know quite a few women in their early to mid-twenties that gravitate towards older men and modern men so don't sell yourself short.

Young startup guys are in the hustle and grind, so it's easy for them to skip a day or two of showering. Startup entrepreneur types can usually work anywhere in the world, and in the beginning, it might just be in their tiny little apartment with their dog, and their dog may be OK with a few days without a shower, but the women he's meeting… uh, not so much.

They pop out of their cocoon to grab a few beers with the fellas and they've got a beard and nasty nose hair, not a good look. Women can smell it a mile away if your man parts smell like sweat or your suit smells like mothballs.

In my profession, I assist my clients with styling and image consulting, though I won't dive too deep here because I cover more stuff in the chapter on style. Just know for now, having charisma and an exciting dating life is absolutely about how you look, which connects with how confident you feel.

FAME. If you have fame you have a charisma power trait. With fame comes power, status, and possibly money. Fame is sexy. It is an alluring social capital.

Women enjoy being in the company of a famous man. Some women are turned on just by a famous man touching them. If a woman aspires to do something in an industry and she believes a famous man can help her or make her more popular, this will make her even more eager to be with this famous person. Some women feel like it makes them something special just to be able to sleep with a famous man.

Even a down-and-out celebrity who is penniless can still pull women if he has a claim to fame, even if it's former fame.

I have a friend who shall remain nameless. He used to be a famous actor in Hollywood. If I mentioned his name you'd know him and the parts he played. When he was at the height of his fame he had a line of girls waiting around the corner everywhere he went.

In the looks department he's average, never an actor known for his looks. He played a lot of bad guy roles because he looked the rough part. These days his acting career is washed up and drinks like he has stock in a liquor company.

Do you think his love life has dried up? Not hardly. He's much older, much rougher looking and still has the pretty young girls who flock to him, something that the average guy could only hope for.

He's still a nice guy, albeit an alcoholic with no real money, no real looks, and not a big talker, but he still has the power of fame from a long time ago.

The bottom line is that fame can make even the ugliest man attractive and your fame will precede you. Fame is like the Energizer bunny, it keeps on ticking long after the ticking has stopped.

Fame is a form of capital and there are a lot of ways that even the average guy can get it. You can acquire it by hanging around a famous person, being part of their entourage if you will. Entourages get just as much interest from women to a certain degree as the famous person.

The rock band might get the first pick, but think about all those lovely rejections. However, let me be clear - a high-quality woman won't just be attracted to you only because you have a high POWER trait; you need more quality attributes.

You can also acquire fame by getting a celebrity or famous person to vouch for you. For example, if you are hanging with a successful guy in the start-up world and he vouches for you. Let's say you created this new app and it's amazing, although it hasn't made you any money yet, or made you famous. Still, Elon Musk is a big fan and he shouts out your app on an Instagram - watch your fame capital increase.

NO POWER (TRAITS), NO PROBLEM

But let's pretend your power traits are not that strong or nonexistent. This could mean you don't have money, but you have a job that pays you well. You aren't a looker, but you have attractive traits so there are plenty of women who will be attracted to you, especially if you have other qualities.

Remember the first survey and the qualities that both men and women want - kindness and understanding. When a man shows a woman kindness and understanding he makes her feel special (important and valued), and it goes both ways. Think about how you feel when you meet a kind woman, one who understands or "gets" you.

The next quality that makes dating exciting for women is finding someone with an exciting personality. No woman likes a bore, not on a date and certainly not in the bedroom. When you excite a woman, you mesmerize her and it goes back to a man who has a woman who it appears treats him like a King. If you want to be treated that way and have an exciting sex life, up the excitement.

Ah, intelligence. Women love an intelligent man and this isn't about how many degrees hang on your wall or your highest level of education, although a highly educated man is a complete turn on.

But more so than intelligence is emotional intelligence. Emotional intelligence in a nutshell is common sense. Certain words or themes that are so important to have charisma and an exciting dating life are so key, like emotional intelligence you'll see me bring them up several times in this book.

Let me ask you a few questions:

Are you good at listening to others?

Are you good at or at least able to make yourself be heard but not in a rude way?

Are you able to forgo the poker face and show some emotion?

Are you able to filter your emotions for each situation?

Are you able to relax your RBF (Resting Bitch Face) and appear to be smiling when no one is watching?

Can you show a little warmth?

Can you give attention?

Can you be confident?

Are you able to use some "UP" body language? (head up, smile up, eyes up, hands up) (you'll look fun, feel fun)

Can you maintain eye contact without looking creepy?

Are you good at reading between the lines (facial cues)?

Take an extra few minutes to say goodbye or hello?

Do you have presence?

A curiosity?

A follow-up?

Are you able to connect with people who are different from you?

Do you know how to give the appropriate touch?

Do you have a way with adjectives?

If you can tick off yes to a few of the above questions and confident that you can say yes to even more with a little assistance, then there's hope for you in the charisma department even if you don't have the POWER TRAITS. If you are willing to venture out of your comfort zone just a little then there is even more hope for you in the charisma department.

LET'S DO AN EXERCISE

Think of someone who you consider to have charisma. What makes them charismatic? For this exercise don't use things from the POWER LIST. OK, who did you name and why? What do they have that you don't? Write the first word that comes to your mind – what's the first one that comes up?

Who did you name and were they a celebrity, politician, or ordinary guy?

Whomever you name from the above list, write down what

makes them charismatic. Are there other things you can think of that make them likable that are not on the list? If so, write them down.

I'll share more about McGregor and Osteen in a later chapter. Still, for this quick list, I'll use Pastor Joel Osteen. Things that make him charismatic aside from having Power Traits:

He's easy on the eyes

He has excellent body language

He is a great speaker

He is pleasant

He is relaxed

He has a presence

He is well groomed

He projects warmth

He is calm

He appears authentic

I'm not asking you to go gah-gah over a man, but do create your list as a helping tool so you can easily learn to spot what makes someone charismatic when you see it.

You might not be born with a Power Trait, but there are plenty of ways to get a few, if not all. But power traits are nothing without other core attributes that don't cost you anything.

KEY TAKEAWAYS

It's the age-old argument women want men for their money, and men want women for their looks. Sometimes it's true and sometimes it's not. Don't get caught up in this debate and at the very least take it for what it's worth.

A study in the late 80's on "Human Sexual Selection" by psychologist David Buss and Michael Barnes asked people to rank 76 characteristics as it pertained to what they value most in a potential mate. The results of this study listed these top three:

1. Kind and understanding.

2. Exciting personality

3. Intelligence

In other studies men do put looks first and women put money. Again, it's an age-old argument and so what. Roll with what you got.

Some attributes instantly attract women. If you don't have them you can fake it until you make it.

The attributes are money which translates to financial security.

It is power which translates to "independence" and "status". Looks and fame.

No money, become more ambitious and you'll get money. An ambitious person is confident.

Power is all about presence.

You don't have to be the best looking guy in the room but any man can make himself look better.

Fame, get some, or borrow it if you can.

Other attributes play and pair nicely with the power attributes like kindness and understanding, being exciting and intelligent.

I gave a long list of questions that if you can even check off some, you are a stud and don't know it. Next, make a list of someone that has charisma. Why did you put them on the list? What core charisma traits could you identify in them?

CHAPTER 4

SMALL TALK & NONVERBAL COMMUNICATION

The pain of staying the same has to become greater than the pain of change

- Richard Price

THE OTHER DAY I saw the silliest yet cutest t-shirt. The t-shirt was of a bottle of ketchup and a bottle of mustard. One was supposed to represent the man, and the other bottle represented the woman. The slogan read something like he's the ketchup to my mustard or something corny like that.

Corny or not, that's what body talk is to small talk, the ketchup to the mustard. The Ying to the Yang. They're supposed to complement one another.

Once you get how to make verbal language and body language play nicely together, you'll understand how to unlock her legs, her heart, or get what you want in your dating life.

Not only do you have to know how to make forms of communication play nicely, but you also have to be able to read her lips, hear the words coming out of her mouth and understand voice tones.

A famous, often quoted, equally misunderstood, and slightly controversial study by Dr. Albert Mehrabian,

attributes 93% of communication to words not spoken. Here's how the numbers break down:

7% relates to the importance of the words used

38% refers to voice tone and inflection

55% refers to the importance of face and body language

The study created for a specific context some 40 plus years ago still has communication experts in dogfights and disagreeing with the study on the breakdown of its numbers. While some disagree on the breakdown of Dr. Mehrabian's numbers, most researchers agree that nonverbal communication is equally if not more important than verbal communication.

For example, a popular communication's company released a cartoon video with several communication scenarios to prove that what we say matters more than a mere 7%. It's an interesting video, and I'll share the YouTube link on how you can watch it at the end of this chapter.

In one scenario a male cartoon character, I'll call him cartoon man, flashes his eyebrows, lifts his eyes, flaps his arms and then hump-haunches his shoulders.

The narrator in the video asks viewers to try to determine what cartoon man is communicating. Of course, it's impossible to know.

Next, cartoon man gets a bit more dramatic. He puts his hands behind his back, humps his shoulders (humps not haunches, there's a difference) as he flashes his eyebrows, makes movements with his eyes, wiggles his lips releasing unintelligible throat groans, but never opening his mouth.

Probably if a study group were convened to guess what cartoon man was trying to communicate with his throat groans, facial expressions, and gestures, the guesses would be all over the place.

I suspect you'd get guesses everything from - he's confused about something, lost, or needs to be committed to a mental institution. My guess would be he's horny as hell. It's impossible to know what cartoon man is trying to communicate.

The next segment of the video shows a cartoon boy begging his cartoon mom for a dog. Cartoon mom tells cartoon boy that "maybe" she will get him a dog. But her body language leans more to communicating "Maybe Not."

But then her body language could also be interpreted as yes, she will get him a dog but she's not thrilled about doing so. Although the creators of the cartoon state that her body language is saying "No." Whatever the case, it's their cartoon and if they say she's saying no, then OK.

The next segment in the video shows a big burly cartoon man asking his petite cartoon wife if she's still angry with him.

Petite cartoon wife frowns, folds her arms and says in an angry tone "NO!" Clearly whatever big burly cartoon man did to his petite wife, still has her pissed.

Viewing the last cartoon scenario felt like seeing Dr. Mehrabian's formula in action. Petite's wife's tone, how she says the word "No," the frowning of her face and folding of arms communicates more strongly what she really means.

I'm sure most would guess she's still very angry.

7% relates to the importance of the words used. Petite woman uses only one word "No."

38% refers to voice tone and inflection. Petite woman screams the word "No!" at her burly husband.

55% refers to the importance of face and body language. Petite woman has an expression on her face (and if looks could kill), she folds her arms and refuses to look at her husband.

The last cartoon scenario brings out an important point of Dr. Mehrabian's study that when words and body language don't match up, people believe the body language. When burly man asks his petite wife if she's still mad, her words are "NO" but clearly her actions speak louder than her words and we can infer that she is very angry. (when words and body language don't match up, people believe the body language)

The point the creators of the video are making is that each type of communication is equally important and that those who put too much emphasis on reading body language and little to no efforts on other forms of communication will fail. As an example, in the first cartoon scenario we are unsure of exactly what the man is trying to communicate. In the second scenario the mother says yes, but her body language uh not so much.

The video creator further argues that if body language made up for such a high percentage of communication, there would be no need to learn foreign languages.

I know what you are thinking. Well, hell, if that's the case let's just skip the meaningless small talk and get straight to body talk in the bedroom.

Not so fast, small talk is a social lubricant needed to break the ice in a social dating situation. You need each form of communication to make the dating thing work. Each communication piece must work together to get the results desired, ever heard of the game Escape?

In case you don't know, the Escape game is a physical adventure that takes place in a created atmosphere like a dungeon or a prison. The live adventure is inspired by the "escape-the-room" video game in which players must solve a series of clues to escape one room and get to the next room. The players repeat the process of escaping rooms until they completely escape.

There's a level of premature excitement when players escape one room of clues and move to the next because with each escape they get closer to the final escape. The prematurity comes because escaping one or several rooms does not mean you escape.

Think of the escape rooms like the forms of communication mentioned in the study, each room (forms of communication) builds upon the next. There's no way to master small talk (a conversation) if you aren't using the right tone or body language.

Got small talk, but your tone and body language are off then you won't unlock anything. You'll get through one door, but you won't make it out.

Although many studies conclude that small talk (words used) is less significant than body talk, the latter of which will cover in greater detail in the "Body Talk" chapter, make no mistake about it, small talk is a BIG social lubricant and a big bleepin' deal.

You make small talk every single day and for the most part, it's meaningless. You chat it up with the UPS girl who drops off a package at your office (oh use your imagination!). You chit chat with the persty (perky plus busty equals persty) Starbucks cashier.

Those conversations come easier because you don't usually have an objective except to exchange pleasantries, it's too early in the day for you to have any objectives, isn't it?

You've paid for your package, you're paying for your coffee so what reason would the woman have to do anything but be nice and do her job?

Compare random social settings to the social dating setting in which single people usually chat it up sexily and playfully. Suddenly some men forgot how to make small talk because there's something at stake. Look boring and say the wrong thing and you are going to have a long, uninteresting night.

The key to having an unforgettable night is to approach women with confidence and start off with good small talk. If you are not famous, rich, or good-looking, pretend that you are and go for it. Most women aren't as hung up on looks as men are.

I'm not suggesting that you approach the woman with a mouthful of lies, instead, approach her with confidence and never allow yourself to believe any woman is out of your league.

A woman who is out of many men's league, is not out of yours, not if you know the right way to strike up a conversation and your body language does not read like an apology.

I had a very rich and very handsome client who I successful matched up. Before getting married, he liked his women young, legal and tender. This former client has grandchildren, he's a granddaddy, and granddaddy liked em' legal but young.

Hey, we've all got our vices, for those of you who think an older man being attracted to a much younger woman of legal age is a vice.

This older man who I'll call Donald, before getting married, liked to date young tenderoni's, but he was intimidated by them. He believed their age and beauty made them out of his league. That was the wrong way for him to think since he could still swing a bat (thanks to Viagra) and write a check - he has boatloads of money.

I'm having a little fun here, but regardless of who you are, never allow yourself to think that a woman is out of your league.

Instead tell yourself, lie to yourself if you have to, that no woman is out of your league.

If she's taller than you, she's not out of your league.

If she's the heir to the richest family in the world, she's not out of your league.

If the plastic surgery she's had makes her better looking than 90% of the women you know, she's not out of your league.

You have to tell yourself stuff like that when you are in a social setting and looking to meet a woman.

Some of the women I interact with for matchmaking have told me that they are sick and tired of dating young, broke, and broken men with empty pockets and hearts, and who act as if they've taken an overpriced course from a washed-out "love guru."

This "love guru" has taught them to use laugh out loud ridiculous pick-up lines and ridiculous terminology like "negging," "split and conquer" and the worst of all of them "nobody puts baby in a corner."

That sounds extra creepy.

My intent is not to dog out younger men, who if they are anything like my clients, are successful. It's simply to help you realize any man is capable of having their dating preferences. They are capable of having small talk that is not awkward and boring if they are confident.

A woman can sense a man with no confidence like a dog can sniff tail. If you are nervous and stumble over your words you likely won't get the time of day, and if you do, instead of dropping it likes it's hot, she'll drop a lot of dead air.

If you show confidence in words and body language even if a woman is not interested, you are less likely to have a long boring night. Even if the women at first sight isn't attracted to you if you approach with confidence, even if you get a rejection, it will be done in a way that you won't feel dogged, *"I'm flattered but married."*

But if you approach nervous and weak, you get what you get.

My client Donald should not have been interacting with women with an apologetic body language and small nervous talk in a weak tone.

I'm old enough to be your granddaddy, or I'm some creepy old dude.

Instead, I taught him that his mental state of mind needs to be that no woman is out of his league.

Women are in the blowing business we are not in the blowing you off business. That is to say, we like what men like. We like dating, we like sex, we love romance. We realize that small talk is a necessary step in first getting to know someone.

If you approach a woman and she's rude for no reason, and you have not said anything offensive to her, "hello" is not offensive.

Then she's not the right person for you anyway and you don't even want to sleep with her because she is a little, well never mind. Anyone that barks at you just for saying hello and attempting to start up a conversation is not someone who you want to be involved with.

However, if she says hello and then blows you off nicely don't be offended, don't be a pest, because maybe it's more about her than you. She might be going through something at the moment that you can't fix. You're not a therapist and unless you are at the top of your charisma "A" game, keep it moving.

Another option in a situation like this is you being skilled at reading body language. Her words might be saying go away, but her body language might read please stay.

Because when verbal and nonverbal don't match nonverbal rules.

However, think back earlier when I referenced the cartoon video. Some body language talk is a lot clearer than others. As you develop strong charismatic skills, you'll become better at taking cues.

I'll get more into body language, yours and hers, in the next chapter since both play a role in the success of the other, but for now it's all about small talk.

Small talk boils down to two words used in two different approaches. That's it, two and two. Playful and Sexy Flirty. Flip and Dip. Women love sexy playfulness, and if you can make her laugh you can make her moan, wait till you read that chapter.

Approach #1 FLIP

The Flip approach means to flip the script AKA change the topic if you are getting nowhere with making small talk.

Being good at flipping topics are what's needed when you approach a new girl, you have to know how to say and do the right thing to spark her interest and make her have that initial attraction to you.

When you strike up a conversation with a woman and one topic doesn't work, change the topic. Even if you've gotten her attention, you could do or say the wrong thing and lose it. Know how to recover.

When changing the topic, keep in mind women don't like to be interviewed. Which could come off like an interrogation. Don't immediately try to get up all in her business. Don't ask about her family, school, job, or her town because that's not how you start with small talk.

She probably holds her family and other personal information near and dear and starting out with that information is none of your business. If you are saying to yourself that you wouldn't do that stop and think if you've ever asked a woman if she's married, or does she have a family because you really want to know if she has children.

Try starting the conversation out by saying hello and if she speaks back go into discussing the atmosphere. What is going on around you?

If that gets a favorable response stick there for a while. My former client Donald does not need to try to discuss social media or what he calls Chat Snap. Don't make a fool of yourself by trying to chat about what you think she would like.

Here's a great line that can work for any man, "So what do you like to do for fun when you're not working?" or "*So, what's keeping you busy when you're not out at an event like this?*"

Natural lines like those are good conversation starters and work well to get someone talking about subjects you can flow from easily and learn more about a woman. They get women sharing and laughing and work much better than corny pick-up lines.

A lot of women I know aren't big fans of pick-up lines, but as with everything else there are exceptions, like if they are playful, and done more tongue and cheek.

A 2016 poll from an online rewards company that enables users to earn points by taking surveys had hundreds of people participate in a survey about what they thought about pick-up lines. In all the comments I read through women appeared to have an overall favorable impression of pick-up lines, as long as they were funny and or clever and not really meant to be taken seriously.

Here's how the poll shook out.

What do you think of pick-up lines?

13% I think they are cute

39% I only like them if they are really clever

33% They are always unoriginal and tacky

12% Other (Specify in comments)

My knowledge as a social interaction coach and this poll confirms not all women hate pick-up lines, although the term itself is often associated with an immature person or cheesiness. Frame your mind that a pick-up line is essentially a conversational starter most commonly used by men to pick-up woman to date.

If I could rearrange the alphabet, I'd put "U" and "I" together. Ewwww, so old school cheesy. I know pick-up lines are so 1980's, still, a little humor if tongue and cheek never hurt anybody and especially if you can find a way to add some grown-up-ness to it, great.

The 12% or the other specific comments indicate women could accept a pickup line with humor. Big takeaway, unless being tongue and cheek stay away from disingenuous pick-up lines and strategies.

Good thing I brought my library card because I'm checking you out. Not.

However, having a sense of humor and being playful and fun is so important to dating that I wrote a chapter about it. Now that you know ways to have a lighthearted playful talk, let me share how to be flirty.

How about a little flirty talk? *You have beautiful eyes.* Not.

You always want to be in touch with social norms and rules of society. It's pretty much always accepted if you use humor, but it's important to choose your flirty (sexy) talk wisely. Flirting sexually is like dipping a toe in water. First you dip (test) before you jump in the water.

Rules for flirting:

Stay away from body part compliments when first meeting someone. To some this may be obvious and to some others it might be hard to do especially if she has amazing body parts like her breasts or legs and has them on display.

Let me be real for a minute. If a woman has nice body parts like her breasts whether they are real or not, and she's wearing a shirt that causes her breasts to stand at attention, she is fully aware that she will get noticed. But whether fair or unfair, she may want to be noticed but she does not want to receive a compliment about her breasts because society has conditioned her to think it's inappropriate.

Instead, take notice of things most men won't think to compliment her on. For instance, if a woman has nice hair, eyes, body, she probably hears the same type of compliments more often than she cares to. A woman won't be excited if you compliment her on something she's been complimented for a thousand times this month.

When you flirt you want to make comments that seem genuine and something that shows you are NOT like every other guy.

Try something more like "you have such a cool style about you" or "I noticed the way you carry yourself, you seem like a very outgoing person" etc. Just be sincere and prepared if she asks you to explain which she very well may do.

It's not that a little later in the conversation if it progresses you can't also mention she has a beautiful smile but maybe start with something a little different. Set yourself apart from the get-go.

Approach #2 DIP.

A women's words coupled with her body language can tell you what she wants, and sometimes she wants you to pick her up and take her home. Sometimes she wants you to get lost AKA, Dip.

And sometimes she wants to chat it up, and she's attracted to you.

However, if the spark doesn't hit after you've tried humor and flirting, move on. Don't sit around with dead air. If you've provided a woman with enough topics to spark a conversation and it does not catch fire, move on. On to the next one.

YOU SHY BOY

If you are a shy person, who is single and who does not want to be you've got to mingle. Easier said than done when you suffer from social anxiety.

I'll stress throughout this book that you don't have to do anything that takes you out of your comfort zone, instead prioritize your energy and make every outing count.

Shy guys have more to overcome than men who are naturally outgoing, add this to shy guys suffering from social anxiety, and it can be painful. Although a shy man has more to overcome he can also score bigger because he must actually take action.

"The pain of staying the same has to become greater than the pain of change." This quote at the beginning of the chapter is powerful and can apply to shy guys.

Shy men are most likely to take action because the pain of not having a dating life (staying the same), has become more painful than the pain of change (taking actions to have a better dating life).

A man who is not shy and has a lackluster dating life may read this book and may take no action, not because he does not want to improve his dating life and become more charismatic but because life gets in the way. He's in no hurry to change this situation because every now and again he gets lucky with a woman and that is just enough to keep him from taking action.

If you are a shy guy, chances are you aren't getting lucky, and so the tips and advice I share in this book are your lifelines.

Having a goal when you go out to meet women is a way to

take action, a way to stay focused so you aren't easily distracted by external things. Whereas an outgoing person might thrive in a busy social spot with music and lights, a shy person might be drained by it.

If you have a specific goal for going out, your brain will focus on that goal and not be overly distracted by the other stuff.

Take time and prepare yourself mentally before heading out, do self-talk and mentally tell yourself something like, you are not going to a jungle to be eaten by animals, you are going out to interact with a lovely creature.

Engage in relaxing things before the outing. I can suggest things that are proven to work like taking a walk, reading, working out, meditation, listening to a calming app, but ultimately you know things to do that relax you.

YOUR VOICE TONE IS KEY TO SMALL TALK

You'll recall that Dr. Mehrabian's study assigns a third or 38% importance to voice tone and inflection. In dating, there are two main types of vocal tonality, one that expresses confidence and one that does not.

A confident voice expresses assertiveness and security, meaning you are in control. An unconfident voice sounds weak and expresses nervousness and self-doubt.

In a social setting when trying to meet someone to date and beyond, your tone should be friendly because it makes you more pleasant and also conveys confidence. If you have trouble sounding friendly, smile. This will expand your face and make your tone sound friendlier.

Keep in mind when you change the expression on your face your voice tone will change. If before you leave the house to go out to mingle something is bothering you, it will show in your vocal tone and body language. So unless you can shake off or put on hold whatever's troubling you, you are going to have a long and uninteresting night.

Those that master the art of being charismatic have something in common, and that is they are able to fluctuate their voice tone at the right time depending on the situation and body language. If a woman smiles and turns so that you can see her neck, she may want you to lean and lower your voice so that it sounds sexy.

If you hate the way your voice sounds, practice. It's as simple as getting out a mirror and talking or using your cell phone to record. Another way to practice is to record yourself talking to a friend and listen back. How do you sound and what can you improve upon?

You'll recall that researcher Fox Cabane shares that there are three things a person can do to display instant charisma.

Lower your voice tone

Don't be so quick to nod

Pause a couple of seconds before you speak

When you learn to make nonverbal small talk and body language play nicely together you can expect that your dating life will drastically improve.

KEY TAKEAWAYS

Although Dr. Mehrabian's study assigns a small number value to communication, all communication experts agree words matter a lot. It's not just what you say, but how you say it. Your voice tone matters.

Dating courses and Love Gurus dish out mostly bad advice.

Men are taught to speak (using the tired pickup lines) as everyone else. There's nothing sexy about behaving like a robot copycat.

In the cartoon video example shared a good point was made. If words didn't matter there would be no need to learn a foreign language. You can watch the video here. The link is valid at the time of this publication.

https://www.youtube.com/watch?v=7dboA8cag1M

Small talk is a social lubricant. There is a right and a wrong way to have small talk. She is not in a job interview and you shouldn't be playing detective.

Like in the game of Escape, all forms of communication must play nicely together.

A confident man has the right mindset. He is positive and does not believe any woman is out of his LEAGUE.

If a conversation is not going well Flip (change) the topic. If that doesn't work, don't talk to dead air and instead Dip (leave).

A good conversation between the sexes is playful, sexy, flirty.

A poll reveals women don't mind tongue and cheek pickup lines that are funny and not taken seriously.

If you are Shy you have good odds because more is at stake.

Have a goal when you go out to mingle.

CHAPTER 5

BODY TALK

You talk a good game but I'm watching how you play

– Unknown

IN THE LAST chapter on small talk, I shared the importance of effective verbal communication and why it is important for verbal talk and body talk to play nicely together.

When verbal and nonverbal communication are in sync, non-verbal amplifies the verbal, meaning your words carry a lot of weight.

When what you say does not match with how you behave, your behavior carries more weight. This means your actions speak louder than words. The main point of Dr. Mehrabian's study is that body language carries more weight than verbal language.

When you communicate nonverbally you must do so in a confi-dent and trustworthy manner. Because trust me, a woman can tell if you are not being authentic or truthful. She spots subtle emotional expressions like a laser beam to match your body language with your words to determine your authenticity and your confidence level.

A woman's discernment and gut feelings are what keep her

from getting hurt in dating and in relationships since we think mostly with our heart and not our part.

That which gives intuition also gives uncontrollable emotions (surprise, surprise). Women aren't as good at controlling emotions as men, which is why she proceeds with caution in matters of the heart.

A women's sixth sense comes from her having better bilateral use of her brain. This is the right side of the brain associated with more intuitive perception.

In the cave days before human language evolved women had a lower social status, no manly grunting allowed (grrr...grrr.grrr) only pleasurable moaning (ooooh...ooooh...ummm).

The woman as the lower specimen label carried over into modern day pre-programming. That famous saying that women are to be seen and not heard became internal and women became more attuned to nonverbal cues and body language. The words she may never speak out loud find occupancy in her mind.

Oh, this powerful gift from mother nature reigns especially strong in women who have raised children. Consider the first way a woman bond's with their baby is by nonverbal nurturing behaviors. It doesn't get more nurturing than a mother's breast in a baby's mouth.

Women are also more intuitive because of the difference of grey and white matter in the brain and processing messages from 14-16 different parts of their brain, compared to men processing messages from about 7 parts of the brain.

Having more white than grey matter and processing from more parts of the brain is neither better or worse and it merely explains a woman's strong ability to read body language. This does not mean that every woman is more perceptive than every man or that men don't have intuition because they absolutely do.

Honey, you can read her too.

FIRING OFF THE RIGHT SIGNALS

When a beauty captures your attention so much so that you'd like to meet her, your body language must fire off the right signals.

You want to be attuned to what your body language is communicating. You don't want your body to communicate badly.

You'll recall, Dr. Albert Mehrabian's study attributes a whopping 93% of communication to words not spoken.

The Breakdown:

7% relates to the importance of the words used

38% refers to voice tone and inflection

55% refers to the importance of face and body language

Communication experts may disagree on the breakdown of those percentages, all agree however that nonverbal communication is a powerhouse.

Consider if you are on a date with a woman you've gone out with on several occasions and you are really enjoying her and you have even been hinting over the past few weeks that you'd like to see each other exclusively.

Suppose you are on a date with her and an attractive woman walks by and you take a sneak peek not wanting your "soon to be exclusive" date to catch it but she does. Suppose right after that she says something like "Hey I thought you wanted to be my boyfriend?"

You answer, "I Do" as your eyes travel up the other woman's perfect set of legs topped off with a nice ass. Since when verbal communication is contradictory to nonverbal communication, nonverbal wins.

Your words say yes, but your body language and wandering eyes say otherwise.

Now suppose you turn your body in the opposite direction away from the woman with the nice legs and butt. Then you playfully pull your date in your arms, smile and look directly into her eyes and say something like "Hey I notice a pretty woman, but I only have eyes for you."

In the first example your body language is contradictory to your verbal language. In the second example although your words are a bit overused, your words are congruent with your body language making them more believable.

As a matchmaker and charisma coach, I breathe, eat, and sleep the behavior and body language moves that turn women on or off. You can take what I tell you to the bank and cash it in and cash her out and jumpstart your suffering or non-existent dating life.

As I cover these tips, receive and act upon them. Whether the information is a refresher, has been long forgotten, or completely new - your dating life and other areas of your life will greatly improve as you'll now be aware of body language that turns women on or off.

Never again will you question what to do and what not to do in front of a woman and your dating life will be a heck of a lot better because of what I'm sharing.

Remember a woman can read your subtle moves and big body language too. Sometimes you are conscious of what you are doing and other times maybe not. Allow me to help you improve your body language.

THE BEST BODY LANGUAGE TO EXHIBIT

In no particular order.

GROOMING.

You may question what grooming has to do with body language - the answer - it has everything to do with it since it speaks to how you feel. If you are unkempt you'll feel unattractive and your body language will display unattractiveness.

Being well groomed lets a woman know just how well you take care of yourself, and in some cases, it reveals your level of education and sophistication. Your grooming habits can reveal if you are stagnant or ambitious.

HEALTHY

Health has everything to do with body language. If you don't feel good, chances are you aren't going to look good.

Even if you have the physique you want and you are comfortable with your body weight, squeeze in time for exercise because exercising triggers brain chemicals which are a natural confidence booster.

POSTURE

There is a reason Mrs. Teacher tapped you on the head with a ruler when you were in grade school as she yelled for you to sit up straight. She didn't want you to have sloppy posture and end up with a hunched back. There is nothing more unappealing than a stooping man.

Good posture makes you look taller (if height is a concern), and better (if your looks concern you). I've noticed some men who haunch without even realizing it. Hunching and bending is an unattractive position for a man.

Practice your posture in a mirror. Stand tall, with your feet slightly apart, and arch your back. You are the man!

The right posture can give you a great big presence, one of the key attributes of charisma.

Additionally, good posture is said to make organs function better and in some cases prevent aches and pains.

EYE CONTACT

Always make sure you have good eye contact since doing so makes you connect better with a woman while coming off as powerful and more personable.

If you are able to make good eye contact you'll stand out from the pack of men who are afraid to look a woman they are attracted to in the eyes.

A way to ensure that your eyes are communicating what you want them to is to get a mirror, close your eyes and imagine something that excites you and when you feel exceedingly excited open your eyes and examine closely how they look. See the difference?

STRIDE

When you walk in a place full of beautiful ladies take big steps and take up lots of room, respectfully. A man who commands space commands her attention.

SMILE

I love the benefits of smiling which produce pleasure feelings in your body. When you smile the D.O.S.E neurons are released. I call the D.O.S.E, the healthy happiness drugs.

Dopamine is the pleasure transmitter and produces feelings of confidence and happiness, it has been compared to a natural cocaine.

Oxytocin gives you a massage and relaxes your muscles.

Serotonin improves self-esteem and produces a mild euphoria.

Endorphins are a natural painkiller that has a positive effect on mood.

TOUCH

Use your hands to make appropriate and friendly gestures. Do not fidget or tap on your phone because it's rude and makes you appear insecure or unfriendly.

Practice, Repeat and Conquer

If you take no action on these tips you get no action, translation, your dating life will continue to suffer. Don't be shy about getting in front of a full-length mirror as you practice each tip shared.

I'll sometimes help a client go through the last 5 tips shared. I'm often told by my clients that they feel immediately better.

FAKE IT UNTIL YOU MAKE IT

I teach my clients that when they go into a social setting to fake it until they make it. This isn't' about being fake as much as it is about projecting confidence.

When you walk into a bar or nightclub you should do so with confidence. Especially if you've been exercising (feel good) and are well-groomed (look good). Congratulations for starting out on the right foot.

Now walk in the place like you own it. Don't be rude, be friendly and cool. Remember a woman can read your subtle as well as your big moves.

Take big steps and take up a lot of space so you seem confident. Never scurry or take little tiny feminine steps. As you walk in shake hands with others and flash that D.O.S.E smile.

Act like you know people and like people know you. "Hey man, how's it going man?" Hey, haven't seen you in a while." What's up dude?" "Hey good to see you." Whoever you shake hands with give them a good handshake and make eye contact.

Go up to the bar and stand using good posture while ordering a drink, as you greet servers, staff and complete strangers with a smile.

You'll notice that the minute you order a drink women will be more open to talking and opening up to you. Not because they want a drink, but because they are curious as to who is this popular and friendly guy.

Popular guys get noticed by women and they seem approachable. Want to know who else gets noticed? Men who go out with one or several attractive women. Ladies want to know who is the popular guy with the flock of attractive women.

Acting popular will boost your confidence 10-fold and it's a lot better feeling than standing at the bar like an apology lusting after women.

There may be people in the place who you spoke to who think, "Do I know this guy?" OR "Who the hell is that guy?" Who cares?

Nobody is going to call out the popular guy that everyone likes. They are glad to know you, although they really don't know you.

In the slight chance someone calls you out you can state

that you thought they were someone else, then smile and keep it moving.

If you act sociable and friendly you will attract women. I will stress as I have throughout this book that the key above all else to being charismatic is not straying away from who you are. Faking it is not about being fake, it's about being clever and on a constant improvement quest to kickstart or spice up your dating life.

MENTAL DISCOMFORT

You've learned the moves to make and how to fake it until you make it. Last chapter I covered having a goal when you go out so you won't be as easily distracted by external factors.

Having a goal will also help you deal with mental discomfort. You absolutely want to avoid MENTAL DISCOMFORT beforehand by eliminating anything upfront that might cause you to appear uncomfortable.

The way to conquer mental discomfort in addition to practicing is to be prepared. There is a reason a woman carries a purse, a purse doubles as her survival bag. I'm not telling you to carry a purse, although keeping a survival kit in the car is not a bad idea.

For instance, you might get a headache when you are out and you don't want to be bumming Tylenol in front of, or from a woman. You might have something going on physically at the moment like allergies or stomach issues, keep something in your car to take care of that.

I was out once with a few friends and a man asked my girlfriend if she had anything for a headache. I didn't think much of it but after the guy left my friend jokingly asked if he needed pain medicine because he was on his period.

A little crude sense of humor but women engage in locker talk like men and you don't want to do anything in front of a woman which makes you appear weak or helpless.

Beyond keeping a survival kit in your car (if you drove and didn't take an Uber), make sure you are relaxed before you go out. You can relax by going for a walk, sitting quietly for a few minutes, or use a meditation app. My favorite app is the free Insight Timer Meditation App which works well as a stress reducer.

There are many free Apps that you can use to help you relax but this one because it includes types of guided meditation exercises to help you deal with stress.

When you're out do stop by the little boy's room and not just to pee. Check your appearance. If you have hair, is it still in place? Is your zipper up? No food stains on teeth or clothing? Is breath fresh? Even if your breath is fresh, pop a mint anyway for a fresher mouth feel.

HOW TO READ HER BODY LANGUAGE

Now that you know how to improve your body language let's discover how to read her body language to determine how she's feeling and if she's interested in you. Some men think they know all there is to know about a women's body language and they really don't.

It never ceases to amaze me how many men will continue to ignore a woman's rather obvious attempts to show them they are not interested. You can usually spot it time and time again in any night spot on any given night anywhere in the world.

If she's not interested in you she'll do everything she can to avoid eye contact. She might look around as if she's looking for someone to rescue her.

This is a woman saying that she is not interested in you in a friendly way. If you hang around too long she may become unfriendly. She may begin to frown, text, or let out audible huffs that suggest you are annoying.

If her body language is open and she appears on the fence about you, you might try to flip (change) the conversation. If after that she remains dry or there is dead air, you don't want to hang around and be a douche, instead dip (leave).

If a woman is attracted to you she may move into your private space and she may even touch you. She will smile at you. She may twist her body around in an attempt to show you her best attributes or how sexy she looks in her outfit. She may begin to mirror your movements.

If you smile and speak to her she may hold her head down as she smiles back and bats her eyes. She may turn her head to show you her neck as if to say, come closer and smell me. She may play with her hair.

Sometimes reading a woman's body language can be tricky because her superpower is an advantage and disadvantage. The same chemical that makes her process stuff differently than men also acts to make her more emotional and insecure. Emotional and insecure women sometimes have the same body language as women who are not interested.

Her nervous behavior could be misconstrued as being uninterested. You'll recall in the *Dating Decoded* chapter I discussed the reasons for a woman's nervousness which could be everything from being jealous that you will pick her friend over her, to thinking you won't get to her before she has to leave.

When out looking to mingle you'll run into all types of women who have as many different behaviors as they have outfits. You'll run into insecure women, confident women, and stuck up women. Confident women usually aren't rude, stuck up women usually are.

They have a self-perception problem and think they look better than they really do.

Stuck up women have a long list of qualities that they want in a man and although you meet them, she'll find some reason in her shallow mind as to why you don't. Don't even waste your time with her, you can find a confident woman that acts nicer and looks better.

A woman who is insecure although she's attractive may send off stand-off ish messages but you'll see little clues from her.

If you have brought your "A" game, which you have since you strolled in the establishment like a "boss", she will probably speak first and if she does not, then you speak and begin the small talk.

As you two chit-chat she may begin to flirt with you to show that she is interested.

That's a best-case scenario, the worst-case scenario is that no one notices you and you must be the one in pursuit. Chances are this is the most likely scenario.

Let's go back to the guy strolling through the establishment like he owns the place, full of confidence. He lands at the bar, grabs a drink and notices a hot woman sitting at a table all by her lonely self.

He hesitates to approach because her body language suggests she does not want to be bothered. Her hands are folded across her body and she's frowning like she is ready to leave.

Let's stop right here. A man should not be intimidated by her demeanor if she's the one he wants to get to know. If he likes her he has to approach her immediately using the 3-second rule. He has just a few seconds from the time he is presented with an opportunity to meet her to take action.

This is powerful. The 3-second rule is effective because if you wait any longer your inner critic will jump all over you and begin pumping self-doubt into your brain. If you see a woman you like, immediately approach her.

Back to the story. The guy strolling through the establishment grabs his cojones and goes for it because the woman sitting by herself even with the unfriendly expression on her face looks like a Goddess. Like if he hooked up with her she is capable of taking him somewhere magical. He's confident because he knows that women visit social establishments for the same reason men do.

He approaches and wouldn't you know it she's even more beautiful up close.

This is where I must stop this story again because this is where the guy will either freeze up or man up. If he freezes up he approaches her like an apology. If he man's up he approaches her like no women is out of his league.

If she looks like she has been sculpted from golden clay, she's not out of his league.

If her lips look like they are created especially to do magical things, she's not out of his league.

If her eyes are more beautiful than the brightest star, she's not out of his league.

Keep in mind (although it may be hard to) that her looks are only a small part of the package. That's where guys get in trouble. Everything they think about the woman at the moment is tied to how good she looks and it really shouldn't be. If you can take your focus off her looks and get into the conversation and ready her body language you will be much more at ease.

The guy must read her body language to know if she wants to get lost or get laid. If she's bored and interested or bored and uninterested. Is she glued to her phone? Is she frowning or smiling or looking around the room while you're speaking? Pay attention to these things.

Relax and ask friendly non-threatening questions like what has brought you out this lovely evening? If she puts down her phone and smiles, you're on the right track! You are warming her up.

If she gives a friendly answer and the conversation begins to flow that's a good sign and you want to keep watching her body language for additional clues.

A FUN EXERCISE

There is this TV show and you may have heard of it. It's called *Impractical Jokers.* If you aren't familiar with the program, it's a show about four comic friends who challenge one another into doing public pranks, each trying to one-up the other.

It's a funny show where they try to convince unsuspecting, random people to do things for them. I saw an episode of one of the guys walking around in a grocery store with a woman on a leash, asking random people to hold on to her while he went to go find something in the store.

The different reactions from the random people in the store were hilarious and also very surprising what the guys got away with. This is a great show to watch to study the art of reading body language. You'll see plenty of times on the show when one of the guys says the most ridiculous thing, yet his body language suggests he's as serious as a heart attack and people fall for the prank hook, line and sinker.

Just remember the importance of being able to read her body language is a must if you are to excel in attracting high caliber women. Don't forget it's not only her body language YOU'RE watching but she is watching YOURS as well.

There is a reason that well-renowned researchers like Dr.

Mehrabin and others assign such a high percentage in their studies to body language. It's that important!

KEY TAKEAWAYS

Actions speak louder than words.

Women have a superpower that enables them to read body language very well, including the subtlest of expressions.

Women and men process things differently in the brain. It's neither better or worse, just different.

Firing off the right signals to women is crucial. Your body language should project confidence.

Best Body Language To Exhibit:

Be well groomed.

Take good care of yourself.

Have good posture.

Make eye contact and smile.

Stride (walk with confidence), and take up space in a friendly way.

Touch in a non-threatening way and use your hands to make appropriate and friendly gestures. Do not fidget.

Practice & Repeat. Take no action. Get no action

Fake it Until You Make it when you go into a night spot. Act confidently as if you are well connected. This is a sure-fire way to attract women.

Conquer mental discomfort by being prepared.

Learn to read her body language to improve your dating life.

CHAPTER 6

CHARISMATIC LISTENING

Be careful of your thoughts, for your thoughts become your words. Be careful of your words, for your words become your actions. Be careful of your actions, for your actions become your habits

- Chinese proverb

ONE PIECE OF advice I often give to men looking to improve with women is to start doing active listening. Active listening is all about building a strong rapport.

If a man is able to better listen to a woman, he is able to build a deeper connection. Men who possess exemplary listening skills score higher charisma points than those who don't.

Imagine an attractive woman is sitting at a table by an outdoor café. Her name is Joan. Joan's beautiful sundress and flawless hair are blowing wildly in the wind.

There is a man seated across from Joan. His name is John. John is listening to Joan intently as she speaks.

Joan: *"I love this time of year, when the summer is leaving, and the fall is arriving. The weather is perfect; it's neither too hot nor too cold. Fall is my favorite season because it* *encourages me to be productive. Weekend mornings during the fall are the best."*

As Joan speaks, she leans towards John. John mirrors her movement and leans towards Joan, making eye contact and smiling as he speaks.

John: *"What's not to like about summer weather?"*

Joan: *"I'm not saying I don't I like summer. What I'm saying is that I love fall because it brings out the best in me."*

John nods and smiles. This time he has listened carefully to what Joan has said. He waits for the right moment to comment and when it comes, he continues:

John: *"What is it about fall that magnifies your energy levels?"*

Joan places her left hand on the table in the same way John's left hand is positioned on the table. The scene and conversation I've described above is a man actively listening to a woman. Not only is John an active listener, he's paying close attention to Joan's verbal and nonverbal communication.

John is present in the moment and it shows in the way he mirrors her body language. As she leans in, so does he, all while preparing to respond to what Joan has said.

There would be telltale signs if John was absent in the moment; signs that any woman using her gift of perception could easily detect. His eyes would be wandering, or he would be fidgeting with his hands or phone.

I mention presence often because it's a key attribute of charisma. Being present in the moment in the scenario mentioned above means that John is paying rapt attention to the beautiful woman in front of him. While he is cognizant *of* the environment around him, he is not, while conversing with Joan, *in* that environment. Nothing going on around John is distracting him from Joan.

John is not thinking about stuff he has no control over currently. On any given day there are a thousand different things that you need to get done, with some things being more important than others. Do not allow those things to mentally extricate you from the moment, however; when you're out on a date, there isn't a damn thing you or anyone else can do about the things in your life that cause you stress or concern.

The situation John finds himself in is a pleasant one. It would be quite foolish for him to ruin it.

Being present in the moment connects you (in order) to: your concentration; better communication; your innate charisma; and finally, to a wonderful dating life. Simply put, John isn't concentrating on any issues that aren't within his power to resolve now.

Let's up the ante. John may be thinking about an upcoming business-related problem. Unless he can take steps to immediately remedy that problem he should forget about it for the time being, unless the problem will bring about a life or death situation if left unchecked.

As for right now, John is on a date with Joan, the type of woman John only hooked up with in a wet dream.

I've shared previously that a woman's perceptiveness allows her to read the subtlest facial expressions. If John is absent in the moment, rest assured she will notice. It is tempting to ignore drifting off during a conversation as being inconsequential. Whatever you do, resist this temptation!

Trust me when I say this: everything adds up, and everything matters. Being present intermittently, or even worse, pretending to be present is appalling and discourteous.

Listening and being present in the moment is a pretty big deal.

It improves the quality of all your social interactions and that's crucial. Being present in the moment reduces anxiety, which is good because, well, how effectively can you really listen to someone while feeling anxious or experiencing bouts of anxiety around her?

John's undivided attention to Joan encourages her to continue speaking and disclose personal information so that he can learn more about her.

Joan now leans in to speak. John puts his arm on his chair's armrest and she does the same. They smile at each other and make eye contact. They are moving into each other's personal space. They are flirting and mirroring each other's body language.

Studies in synchronous body language show that men find women who mimic each other's body language more attractive and they also feel a greater connection. This was also the conclusion of a study conducted in 2009 by French researcher and seduction expert Nicolas Gueguen.

The scene between John and Joan illustrates John using what I refer to as 'the win-win formula' for ACTIVE listening. Learn this formula then tweak it to suit your needs. In doing so, you'll discover whether the attraction and mirroring of behavior is natural. Next, prove that you are listening, then provide feedback. It's a winning combination: Listen actively, pay attention, give feedback. It seems so obvious yet so few actually do it well.

The most effective way of showing that you are paying attention to a woman is by maintaining eye contact. This is the best nonverbal way to express that you are present in the moment and are listening deliberately. Do not stare or glare though so you don't look creepy.

Your eyes should show that you are compassionate and genuinely interested in what is being said to you. On the other hand, wandering eyes will make you appear nervous and uncertain of yourself. You can also show that you are listening by nodding your head occasionally, or by leaning in closer and smiling where appropriate.

In the case of John and Joan's conversation, a smile is appropriate because she's sharing something that makes her feel lively and energetic; the changing of seasons. If she were sharing that she feels lousy whenever summer transitioned to fall, a look which denotes empathy would be more appropriate than a smile. Again, it seems obvious but so few do it correctly.

WHAT'S IN A SMILE?

Women are far better than men at picking up on subtle facial expressions. If your smile is disingenuous, she'll know. If your mind is focused on something contextually irrelevant, she'll know.

A genuine smile confirms you are present in the moment and it's sometimes called a 'Duchenne smile,' named after the 19th century French physician Guillaume Duchenne. Duchenne was a trailblazer in his study of the physiology of facial expressions, which earned him the nickname 'the Smile Doctor.'

Whenever you smile, you potentially activate two muscles. The first is the zygomaticus muscle, which controls the corner of your mouth. A smile which activates this muscle is considered fake.

A genuine smile is produced by activating the muscle known as the *orbicularis oculi*; a muscle which connects our eyes sockets to our mouth. In other words, when it comes to smiling: go big, or go home.

To practice smiling genuinely, you can try a simple exercise of placing something such as a pencil or chopstick between your teeth. Do not touch the selected item with your lips and don't drop it. If you believe this exercise is silly then I'll go ahead and deduct some charisma points from you.

An action not taken is an action wasted. Each action is one which culminates to a genuine smile. Every action you attempt (no matter how minuscule) will help improve your charisma and expand your dating life.

You further show that you are paying attention by offering feedback or asking questions, which you can accomplish by repeating or paraphrasing what was said. Repeating what you have heard is critical. You may be listening but you may not have heard correctly, or you may have heard what you wanted to hear.

When you repeat what a woman has said back to her it gives her a chance to thank you for being attentive and/or to clarify her point(s), if you haven't repeated it back to her correctly.

You'll recall in the above scenario that John at first repeated what he thought he heard Joan say. Rather than making guesswork out of what she said, John could ask her one or many questions designed to enable him to contribute to the conversation in a meaningful way.

John: *What is about this weather not to like?*

Joan clarifies.

Joan: *No, I said, I'm saying, I like the summer, but I absolutely love fall weather because it brings out the best in me.*

The fact that John misunderstood what Joan said about the weather the first time is trivial. Remember that in their scenario they are sitting outside of a café and it's windy. There could be other external factors making it difficult to hear her, like other people conversing or passing motor vehicles.

It would be problematic for John to repeatedly misconstrue what Joan was saying, even if you factored in the external stimuli that makes it difficult to hear a person speak while outdoors. I'll explain what John could do about external stimuli shortly.

ACTIVE LISTENING: THE WIN-WIN FORMULA

When you are actively listening, you are considering each manifestation of communication: words, inflection, facial cues and body language. These give you a complete picture of what is being conveyed when they're combined and they indicate that you are present in the moment.

Here's the win-win formula in three steps.

Step 1: A woman tells you about something she is feeling.

Step 2: You ask her why she feels that way.

Step 3: You paraphrase or reiterate her statement(s).

Joan's hair is blowing as she turns in John's direction. She gently touches her neck, bats her eyelashes, then says:

Joan: *"I love the time of year between summer ending and fall beginning. The weather is perfect; it's neither too hot nor too cool. My ideal days are the days where I'm able to be super productive. Weekend mornings are the best. I like to make breakfast, get a little work in, a little sex in, a little exercise in."*

In the above paragraph Joan throws out a few interesting clues about herself. She supplements this information using her body language to emphasize what she likes. She's even flirting with autoerotic touching! Autoerotic touching is when you touch yourself in an intimate place where you'd like to be touched by someone else. Joan is indirectly letting John know that she is physically attracted to him.

The next part of the win-win formula is for John to ask a follow-up question for clarity. He should interrupt only when in his estimation it feels right to do so. It would not necessarily be optimal to wait until after she's finished speaking to then speak. If John waits too long, the conversation could go in a completely different direction.

John: *"Why does fall bring out your best energy more so than other seasons? Why does it turn you on?"*

Joan: *"The colors are sexy. The weather is perfect. It brings my energy level up and turns me on. I have more energy to complete goals and to accomplish my work."*

Since Joan is obviously flirting and inviting John to touch her, he could initiate physical contact by, for example, pushing her hair away from her face, gently touching her neck and running his fingers down the small of her back.

John: *"There's something enthralling about a woman who's open about being invigorated sexually, creatively and professionally."*

John is nailing it in this scenario! Even though it's a windy day, Joan's back is facing an open area and there's heavy foot and automobile traffic which makes it difficult to hear Joan, he is reaping success with her.

If the external stimuli becomes excessive and John can't concentrate, he could suggest going inside the café or moving to a less busy location. To be fair, it is hard for some people to concentrate on one another in busy areas.

A good way to reduce distractions is to go places where the people look and behave like you. What do I mean by that? An upper-scale place attracts a different vibe and a different breed of person than a middle-scale place.

DISTRACTED BY BEAUTY

Beauty can be a huge distraction. Some (but not all) men are intimidated by attractive women and the nervousness they experience can stop them from being present in the moment.

Talking to an attractive girl should be no different than talking to anyone else because:

If a woman drops pretty petals off her ass as she walks because she's just that good looking, she's not out of your league.

If she is as beautiful as a rare diamond, she's not out of your league.

If her looks could start a war between countries, she's probably out of your league!

You've doubtlessly seen at least one TV show or movie with a man tripping over himself while interacting with a drop dead gorgeous woman. In the late 70s and early 80s there was an American TV show called 'Threes Company,' for which entire storylines were written around the protagonist, Jack Tripper, being nervous and doing goofy stuff in the presence of attractive women. That storyline and jokes about Jack Tripper tripping over beautiful women worked time after time because stunning women do in fact make some men nervous.

A research study published in the *Journal of Experimental Social Psychology* (a peer-reviewed publication that specializes in social psychology) involved the measurement of brain function in 40 men. The men were asked to complete a memory test, after which they spent several minutes talking to either a man or an attractive woman. The study revealed that the men who spent even a few minutes with the attractive woman experienced a decline in mental performance, thereby yielding less accurate test results.

It's hard to pay attention when you're nervous. Your nervousness could be set off by the women's attractiveness, or by external or internal stimuli. Whereas external stimuli are factors which form part of your surroundings, internal stimuli comprise of how you feel on the inside. This internal discomfort can be caused by any number of reasons, whether past or present, such as a traumatic childhood, unrequited love, or even how you feel on a given day. Maybe your inner critic is being extra critical.

Things that bother you on the inside can affect your behavior. If your internal confusion gets the better of you it can set off a chain reaction; you sweat profusely, you begin to tremble and show some other signs of anxiety. Your mind begins to race. Instead of being present in the moment you aren't listening at all anymore, and when you speak, it comes across as being contemptuous.

Here is a rephrasing of the Chinese proverb at the beginning of this chapter:

Be careful of your thoughts... ("She isn't "feeling" me...")

...for your thoughts become your words... ("Why does she not like me?")

...be careful of your actions... (not making eye contact, slouching, fidgeting, bad posture)

...for they become habit... (one bad date after another)

...be careful of your character... ("You see that guy? He's undateable!")

...for it becomes your destiny (no date, no mate).

The most important thing to know about external or internal stimuli is that most of it is within your control. Don't go on a date at a time or place which puts you at unease. Do everything you can beforehand to prepare and prevent internal discomfort.

LISTEN UP!

In your quest to become more charismatic, more dateable and a better listener, it will help if you attune yourself to your personality type. Are you an introvert, extrovert or ambivert? You may believe that if you're shy you'll have a harder time becoming an active listener because your shyness causes your eyes to wander, causes you to fidget, and/or do other unappealing things.

You can treat your shyness as a disadvantage or an advantage. The advantage with shyness is that it puts you in a position where remaining the same (poor dating life or no dating life) is less sensible than improving yourself for the better (overcoming shyness, learning tips to improve your dating life, etc.).

As a shy person whose desire to change is mightier than his desire to remain the same, you're eager to implement changes in your personality. This is your advantage because it will increase your likelihood of doing things that will improve your dating life, such as being present in the moment or becoming a better listener.

Being shy is not the same as being an introvert. A shy person finds difficulty in composing himself in social contexts, whereas an introvert is energized by solitude. However, a person can be both shy and introverted.

An introvert might find mingling and dating a tad troublesome in the presence of external stimuli which drain an introvert's energy. It's admittedly hard to be present in the moment or to listen if your energy level is being zapped.

An **extrovert** is totally comfortable in any location where the energy and external stimuli are flowing. Extroverts aren't shy. Being in places with a wealth of activity and noise excites them. Extroverts I find have a harder time than the other types.

It may surprise you but if I had to pick among the three personality types mentioned above and decide which may be the least successful for dating, it would be an extrovert. Extroverts opine that because they thrive in high octane situations, they don't need to practice with women. They believe they're perpetually present in the moment and that being a good listener is not one of their problems.

I worked with a particular client who was an extrovert. It was his outgoing personality and confidence in most settings that caused him to strike out frequently with women. The reason is that he didn't follow my advice on improving his dating life. His extroverted nature made him a little cockier than others and it took him longer than most to figure out what he was trying with his dates was not working.

An **ambivert** is a balance between an introvert and extrovert. Ambiverts have been called 'the lost personality type.' They fall in the dead center of personality types and must constantly mix up their routines. Sometimes they want to be by themselves and sometimes they feel outgoing.

You'd think this was the best personality type, but you'd be wrong. The famed psychologist Carl Jung once said, *"There is no such thing as pure introvert or extrovert. Such a person would be in the lunatic asylum."* This makes sense when you consider that introverts are fine (but would rather not be) in social settings and extroverts have moments where they crave peace and less excitement.

Taking the time to consider your personality type will improve your listening skills and boost your charisma. Charisma is what you feel and what you know about yourself to be true.

If you are an introvert at a crowded concert, it's probably not the best spot for you to ooze charisma and date or meet women. On the other hand, if you are an extrovert, you may be entirely comfortable at a loud concert on a date and the communication will flow nicely.

IMPROVING YOUR LISTENING SKILLS

A good listener is intuitive about when it's appropriate to speak and when it's better to listen. Allow me to indulge in some generalizations (though we all know some of them to be true):

- Women feel the need to express everything and can talk a lot. Be patient.

- Women often feel that men don't care about what they say. Show that you do.

- Never assume that what a woman has to say is unimportant.

- Women sometimes overanalyze things. When they do, bring their over-analysis back to the center.

- Women think men can read their minds. They can't.

- Women won't always react the way you want. Don't get frustrated.

- A woman can be all over the place. You want to listen when you meet her or on a first date, even if you decide after listening to her speak that she is not the one for you.

I hope my generalizations made you smile a little and will make your next date a better one now that you know what you might come up against.

BE EMPATHETIC

You want to hear AND 'feel' what a woman is saying, her emotions and her body language. You're not going to appear empathetic if you really and truly don't give two flying fucks about what she's saying, or if you're in a social setting that is contrary to your personality type.

To show empathy you must first practice listening. Listen for as long as you need to and interrupt when appropriate. Just because some women like to talk doesn't mean you should allow them to ramble without interruption, as this too could be construed as an indication of disinterest.

When you are empathetic you build rapport and this energy transfers between those on a date or mingling.

LISTEN TO BODY LANGUAGE

Don't just listen, observe!

Earlier on Joan was throwing out a little sex talk with words and body language. If you want to get better at listening to body language try an experiment that I conducted with a client of mine. I had this client go out with me so that I could show him how to become better at reading body language.

The only assignment I gave him was to become more observant than usual. We observed a couple of cute ladies talking to two older men. "Where are you from? What's your story?" On the surface these women seemed to be engaged in the conversation. My client said that in the past he would have surmised the men were impressing the women. When he took a step back to observe what the women's body language was saying however, he observed that the women were in fact bored. Their arms were crossed and their body language was standoffish. He noticed that while the guys looked excited, the women certainly didn't.

Later my client and I went dancing. Women couldn't take their eyes off him because he was with me. It's true that women flock to men who have a woman with them. Once I moved away to give off the 'we are just friends' signal, a woman came up to him and started grinding on him on the dance floor.

He noticed that the friend she was with was giving her 'I can rescue you' eyes, but her body language to my client and to her friend made it clear that she was enjoying herself.

The client said that in the past he would have believed the friend and given the woman an out. Now he says the girl he was dancing with kept dancing seductively with him and teasing him with her hair. Her body language (*"I'm interested"*) did not match her friend's body language (*"Hey, do you want me to rescue you?"*)

GET YOUR EARS CLEANED

This is not a sexy subject to include in a chapter as sexy as this one, but believe me when I say the subject matter merits a discussion. I once knew a gentleman who was having a lot of trouble hearing. He went to the doctor and had his ears checked. His ears were fine, but he had a lot of earwax built up. I'll spare you the details of the unsexy (albeit painless) procedure the doctor used to clear the wax that prevented him from hearing clearly.

I'm nevertheless sharing this information with you because it all adds up when you look at the big picture. It's easy and possibly more desirable to focus on the big stuff that you should do to be more charismatic and improve your dating life, but what may be something little may count more and in more ways than you realize at first.

Consider this: Team A and Team B are in the finals. The team that achieves victory goes home with the trophy. Team A is fantastic; they make every big play. Team B is fantastic in the same way, but they also don't miss the little stuff, like fouls and field goals.

A few tweaks can bring your listening skills from good to great. Presence is a cornerstone of good listening. Being present in the moment, connects to your ability to concentrate, connects to your ability to communicate, connects to you being viewed as being charismatic and connects to you having an exciting dating life. LISTEN UP!

KEY TAKEAWAYS

If you want to be a better communicator then become a better listener. Men who have great listening skills score higher charisma points than those who don't.

Takes notes from Joan and John's pretend scenario. John is

present in the moment and listening. He isn't focusing on outside things to which he cannot control.

John and Joan flirt with each other through words and body language, mirroring each other's behavior.

John is using the win-win formula of active listening, paying attention, providing feedback and asking questions.

John smiles a truly genuine, Duchenne smile. He smiles from ear to ear.

Be present in the moment, connect to your ability to concentrate, connect to your ability to communicate, which all connects to you being viewed as being more charismatic and having an exciting dating life.

Women's beauty can make men nervous, especially when they are really beautiful.

External or Internal discomfort in many cases can be controlled, otherwise it will affect your dating life.

Are you shy, introverted, extroverted, or a combination of both, ambiverted? Knowing and understanding your personality type enables you to have a more exciting dating life.

Improve your listening skills by being empathetic and hearing a woman out. Women think and speak differently from men.

Listen to her body language. It speaks louder than her words.

CHAPTER 7

MAKE HER LAUGH
MAKE HER MOAN

If you can make a woman laugh, you can make her do anything

- Marilyn Monroe

ONE OF THE qualities women look for in a man (and *vice versa*) is a good sense of humor (GSOH). Women are attracted to men who are entertaining, fun and can tell and take a good joke. A good sense of humor lightens up the general mood and makes the parties involved feel less tense.

Women are often "hit on" in the dating scene, irrespective of their physical appearance. I use the term 'hit on' because there is a difference between being approached by men and getting 'hit on', which to a woman may feel like she is being preyed upon by a pack of wolves.

Average women are frequently hit on because it's easier for guys to converse with an average woman, or ask her out on a date. Attractive women, on the other hand, intimidate some men. Nevertheless, attractive women are hit on often too because, well, they're attractive.

As you're reading this, you may be saying to yourself, *"I don't hit on women a lot"* (or at all, if your dating life sucks). In fact, as a man you may not seduce women at all, which probably explains why you are reading this book for practical tips on approaching women.

There are men who, after drinking a few shots of liquid courage or on the day they graduate from pickup school, start approaching women in the worst way possible. Guys like that give guys like you a bad name and it's also the reason you must have a GSOH.

Before I delve into why you need a GSOH, you should know (if you don't know already) that women love attention. We put on nice clothes and we do our hair and makeup, even when we are going nowhere special. Women relish in feeling and being made to feel attractive.

I have a friend who goes to the gym way too early and she told me that there are plenty of guys there. You know what she does when she goes to the gym? She puts on a little makeup to look prettier, albeit not in an obvious way.

A woman may wear nice clothes, do her hair and makeup and go to the gym for you, but - and this is important for you to understand - one reason you need a GSOH is that rejection is inevitable, thanks to the guys who try to pick up women the wrong way. It's how you handle rejection that will determine your dating success.

My friend shared this story with me: one day while at the gym early in the morning, a decidedly average man walked past her; no muscles or anything esspecially attractive. He made eye contact with her and said, *"I didn't know pretty girls like you came in here this early, I have to start coming in earlier,"* or words to that effect.

My friend said that after he made that comment, she gave him the side eye and smiled as he winked, smiled back and walked out of the gym.

She said he caught her on a morning where she was feeling tired and wasn't in the mood for someone to be flirting with her, which is why she gave him a smirk-smile.

She was charmed by his good sense of humor and didn't feel hounded by him after seeing him a couple more times at the gym. She told me they eventually hooked up and had a couple of brief rendezvous. It didn't work out but she still sees him at the gym and they're cool with one another.

Having a GSOH helped that guy score and it can help you too.

Let's say you are out at a night spot and an attractive girl walks in. She immediately catches your eye and if you're feeling confident that night you might approach her. You do that because you want to express your interest first before other men see her. You want to 'claim' her first.

In this situation she'll likely appreciate that you acknowledged her and showed interest because, again, women love attention. After you approach her, things could go in a number of directions. In a perfect scenario, she'd have a seat at a table with you and give you her undivided attention.

More than likely however, there are other considerations. She could be married or have a boyfriend that she's meeting there (which she may inform you of). It could also be that she wants a minute to sit down and have a drink herself to unwind and take in the surroundings, or wait for her girlfriends to meet with her to help her relax more.

Let's say her response to you is something like a smile followed by the words, *"I'm meeting someone here."* Maybe her body language says, "I'm not interested", or *"I'm not interested right now."*

If you have a GSOH and she does not show much interest when you first approached her, that shouldn't bother you in the least. Sure, she's attractive, but there are many more attractive women than you can shake a stick at.

If you don't want to move on just yet, give her a minute to catch the vibe. Who knows? The stars may align and you two may end up conversing with one another later.

The worst thing you can do in this situation is not have a GSOH and take what's not really a blatant rejection to heart. The rejection isn't blatant simply because you don't know her situation.

She may have told you she was meeting someone there but didn't elaborate on who that someone was. It could be a date or a friend. On the other hand, she could be lying to you; she's not really meeting someone there but she hopes to and needs a minute to relax. Again, maybe she just needs a drink and a little time to soak in the atmosphere.

Don't stare at her across the room all evening and make her uncomfortable. Don't take her ambiguous rejection of you personally and ruin your evening in the process. Don't try to irritate her the rest of the evening in a bid to make sure that nothing for the night goes right for her.

You want to be upbeat and enjoy the vibes of whatever is happening around you. The time you spend worrying about her could be time spent focusing on another attractive lady who is waiting for you to express interest in her.

If you don't have a GSOH, an indirect rejection may bother you. If you do have a GSOH, you'll be optimistic that maybe later she'll come around and if she doesn't, it's her loss, or there's someone better for you on the way, like the lady at the other end of the bar checking you out.

Whatever you do, don't take it personally. Nine times out of ten a woman rejecting you is less (if at all) about you and more about her. Having a positive outlook and seeing the glass as half-full will enable you to better deal with the situation. The best-case scenario is that she'll unwind and may even begin flirting with you. If not, another woman who is checking you out may flirt with you. Believe it or not, women go out to mingle and have fun too. If you put out the right aura in the universe, it will come back to you.

Let's say the stars do line up for you and her or another lady. Just being in an upbeat mood virtually guarantees that whatever happens during the remainder of the evening won't negatively affect you. A good possibility is that the woman you had your sights on (or one that is even more attractive) will come around.

Suppose you are seated at a table and you order drinks. The drinks come to the table, but they're not the drinks you ordered. Consider how a relaxed and chilled guy would handle the situation, as opposed to one who's uptight.

A relaxed and chill guy will be able to take his time to explain exactly what's wrong with the order. He'll ensure that the person taking the order clearly understands what you want. A relaxed and chill guy might even skip ordering at the table and go directly to the bar and pick up the drinks. He's there to have a good time, not be an asshole.

He's emanating good vibes, so the chances increase that what he's putting out will come back to him, such as the correct drinks.

LEVEL 2 DATE OR DATING

Level 2 is for when you get past that first meeting and mingling. Showing her that you have a GSOH will add to what she finds appealing about you.

For instance, if she started dating you and the relationship progressed to the point where one person is giving the other honest opinions on certain things like her/his wardrobe or some other topic, it's going to be important for the both of you to be optimistic. You don't want to date a person or be that person who flies off the handle or sees the glass as half-empty with everything.

I had a girlfriend who dated a guy who was attractive, successful and had many other positive traits, but he lacked a GSOH and pretty much everything pissed him off. If he was stuck in traffic, the glass was half-empty. If he got up in the morning and realized there was no creamer for his coffee, the glass was half-empty. His outlook on virtually every aspect of life was negative.

He probably thought, *"I'm stuck in traffic and now I'm going to be late for a business meeting."* Being stuck in traffic may genuinely suck, but it's not the end of the world. My girlfriend shared with me that he was once stuck in traffic and thought he'd be late for a meeting and kept going on and on about how bad it was going to be, but ended up being on time with a few minutes to spare.

Not only that, but it was an informal meeting with colleagues who knew him well, knew that he was not usually late and would in any event understand and forgive the lateness. Instead of having a GSOH about the dilemma, something as simple as being stuck in traffic would offset his entire day, including his personal time with her.

Think about the kind of woman you want. Do you want some whiny, bitchy lady who is never satisfied with anything and doesn't have a GSOH? You take her out for an evening and let's say one of the heels of her too tight and expensive stilettos snaps off. (Don't laugh... it has happened to the best of us!) She was complaining since she put on the stilettos that they hurt her feet and now she's complaining about the snapped stiletto heel and making a big deal about it, even though she brought along an extra pair of stilettos which she placed in the trunk.

They may not be as sexy, but they are much more comfortable, so the heel of her original stilettos cracking off was to her advantage. No longer does she have to walk around in shoes that would make her whine the entire evening.

If the lady does not have a GSOH, she may ask herself or you, *"How dare the heel of one of my $500 pair of stiletto's break?"* She complains all night and ruins your night; so much so you don't even want to sleep with her anymore.

HAVING A GSOH vs. BEING FUNNY

A person with a GSOH embraces their flaws and the flaws of others in a healthy way. They understand that stuff happens and even when stuff happens that doesn't feel great, like being stuck in traffic, having no creamer for your coffee or having a stiletto heel snap, it's not the end of the world.

A person with a GSOH might be able to tell a joke or two, or can laugh at something about themselves without reading too much into either.

A person with a GSOH can encourage and uplift others and sees the glass as half-full. She/he may not always feel positive, but is always willing to receive positivity. She/he is not a pushover, but when given a choice will often take the high road and drink out of the half-full glass.

Having a GSOH might even mean you tell a good joke occasionally. According to research, women like a good joke every now and then.

There is also research which suggests that having a GSOH is related to sexual selection. Humor is a charismatic trait and humorous people are viewed as ideal candidates for a relationship.

In a small study, a man once told a joke to two friends at a bar while a woman listened at a nearby table.

The man who told the joke was asked to approach the table and ask the woman for her number. Next, the other man who listened to the joke without telling one was asked to approach the same woman and ask for her number.

This scenario was repeated 60 times. The study showed that not only was the man who told the joke three times more likely to get the number when he told the joke, but he was considered more attractive and intelligent.

It's not surprising that the man who told the joke was deemed more attractive and intelligent. Some interesting studies conducted by the University of New Mexico juxtaposed humor with intelligence. In a study conducted in 2011, 400 psychology students were asked to take a cognitive ability test created by researchers at the University.

The students were then asked to write captions for a series of New Yorker magazine cartoons. The captions that were rated funnier were written by the students who scored the highest on the cognitive ability test.

A woman appreciates a man with a GSOH and will be attracted to him, though it's worth noting that having a GSOH is not the same as being funny.

I have two guy friends (yes, I have a lot of friends and clients, I'm a matchmaker, after all). Both of my friends are decent looking; they're not models and are average in the looks department. One friend has a GSOH, whereas the other is always 'on'. He believes that comedians are always 'on', but doesn't realize that this isn't true.

This friend is 'on' non-stop, making girls laugh until they are crying. He is always turning 'everything' into a joke and he's a very funny guy.

He's a very funny guy that women would rather befriend and not date, however. Women describe him as funny and fun to be around, but at the end of the day they see him as a friend at best. This guy, who women routinely prefer to be friends with, does not get that he shouldn't be funny all the time because it comes across as being silly.

The other guy has checks and balances; he has a GSOH, but is not over-the-top with it and isn't always trying to be funny. He'll tell a good joke but he won't actively try to be the life of the party or the center of attention and he has women always attracted to him. They find him humorous, sexy and fun to be around.

Having a GSOH is important but you have to find a balance.

A STICK IN THE MUD

We all know at least one person who doesn't see amusement or joy in anything. One client I worked with has a powerful and intimidating presence. There are tons of powerful people who are reserved and laid back and those qualities make them attractive.

This client however was humorless. Nothing seemed to excite him, not even a beautiful woman. He liked being in the company of a beautiful woman, but women didn't like being around him because he refused to lighten up. He's an attractive, rich and powerful guy, oozing with power traits.

He incorrectly assumed him being who he was and taking a woman on an expensive date was all he needed for her to sleep with, or fall in love with him. Despite his status, women didn't like to be around him because he's perpetually boring and uptight.

I talked to him about lightening up. He replied, "*That's just the way I am. I can't change. I've been like this since I was a kid. They can take it or leave it."* or words to that effect. Put differently: it's his way or the highway.

A research study published in the *Journal of Personality* followed 100 preschoolers from the age of four until their early 20s. At the beginning of the study, the researchers surveyed parents and teachers to categorize their personality as one of three types: over-controlled, undercontrolled or resilient.

The preschoolers categorized as overcontrolled were described as shy, quiet, self-conscious and uncomfortable around strangers.

Those overcontrolled children were generally viewed as excessively controlling their emotions and acting unnaturally or without spontaneity.

The preschoolers categorized as undercontrolled were described as having little to no impulse control, being easily frustrated, and acting aggressively towards others.

The study concluded that even though behaviors may change slightly, the underlying personalities remain the same.

Even though my client's basic personality may be set in stone, there are ways he can adjust his behavior to enjoy a better dating life.

Researcher and author Olivia Fox Cabane has shared that more recent research rejects the notion that a person's basic personality is unchangeable.

My client doesn't think of himself uptight. He thinks his personality is laid-back and reserved. However, women view him as uptight, unkind and undesirable. He firmly believes that even if he were those things, he can't change, but for the sake of a 'good time' he can and definitely should lighten up, smile, and if he's feeling good about himself, tell a joke or two.

If he can lighten up just a bit, he will make the women he talks to feel relaxed, he'll feel relaxed and they can enjoy one another's company.

The way I suggest tossing in a joke is thinking about the profession or field you are in. When I go to see my dentist, he tells the same joke to all his clients. It's something very corny like, *"What did the tooth say to the departing dentist? Fill me in."*

Then my dentist usually points to his mouth where he's had a filling and something even cornier like I did it myself and it didn't hurt.

This is a harmless joke. The first time he told it to me, I laughed. It's an icebreaker. I can hear my dentist when I'm in the chair getting my teeth cleaned telling harmless jokes to other patients. No one minds a harmless joke especially when they're not its subject.

If you want to attract women in a positive way and have them view you as someone who makes them feel good about themselves, you may want to try an ego-boosting joke. Women love jokes which boost their ego.

An example of an ego-boosting joke is, *"You graduated from two Ivy League schools? I was lucky to survive community college!"*

Even if you graduated with a top degree from a prestigious college, the point of the joke is to show that you are impressed with the woman and boost her ego a little.

When telling a joke you never want to make the woman or anyone in her clique its subject. Never tell a joke that could potentially spark a debate. Bear in mind that the point of mingling and dating is to have a good time.

This is not to say that you must walk on eggshells, but until you get past the first meeting and/or the first date, keep it light-hearted. After that and as time progresses you'll explore other areas to see what you two have in common.

HOW TO GET YOURSELF IN A MORE PLAYFUL MOOD

Research confirms that humor improves your overall mood. Humor helps you feel more relaxed on a date. Consider how you'd feel if you had a long stressful day with little to no rest, compared to how you'd feel if you had an exciting weekend after which you woke up refreshed.

When I teach dating and charisma workshops, there are certain things I like to do to crank up my energy level.

I exercise. I drink lemon water. I sit on the beach and absorb the sunlight while soaking in the atmosphere. I'm daydreaming and practicing mindfulness simultaneously. Sometimes I listen to relaxing music. When I have important things to do like meeting with a client or coaching a workshop, I steer clear of all negativity.

I advise my clients to avoid any situation within their control that could negatively alter their mood before going on a date. My advice is that anything negative and relating to your personal life or work be dealt with after the date, not before. This means if dear old sweet Mom wants to chat you up right before your date, but she never shares anything new with you and instead her deep concern for you causes her to nag, or she loves to share negative news with you, don't take the call.

If your business partner is known to bother you during each of your dates with stock or business news that is never positive, don't take the call. Give yourself permission to escape the doom and gloom, if only for a few hours.

I also advise leaving plenty of extra time because unforeseen events can and will occur. For example, your car's tire may be deflated, there may be significant traffic congestion, or someone could argue with you over a parking space. Even if any or all those scenarios were to come to pass, you are early and have enough time to listen to some upbeat music, or to soak in the atmosphere.

I've read stories about entertainers who have their own routines before they go on stage, ranging from eating their favorite candy or drinking their favorite beverage, to exercising or playing backstage with staff. They do whatever it takes to put them in the right frame of mind to remain upbeat and entertain the audience.

If you go out to mingle or on a date, you are doing so to have a good time, meet someone and enjoy the date. This means that if you didn't have a good day you must find a way to put that behind you. Whether the business deal didn't go through, or there's still one lane of the highway to your house and the traffic is a mess, you want to let go of whatever it is that has caused you grief before you go out.

You don't want to be sitting at a bar, drinking like a fish and looking like the world is going to end in five minutes. Don't look like Doug the Downer or exude body language that tells an unhappy story, because it's a huge turn-off.

Not only do you want to let it go for yourself, but you want to let it go for your date. Maybe she's had a bad day too. Maybe it's been a long stressful day at work, or maybe she's in the middle of nursing exams. Whatever it is, people who carry their bad moods with them don't attract other people who can make them feel better.

Norma Jeane Mortenson AKA Marilyn Monroe might have been typecast as a dumb blonde but she was actually one smart lady with an IQ of 168. She understood sexuality and humor and it's safe to assume that she knew the way to unlock a women's legs or heart was through laughter. She loved a man who could make her laugh as do all women.

KEY TAKEAWAYS

Women like men with a GSOH. They do not like men who prey on them.

Women like to look good and they like men who pay attention to them, it's why we wear make-up to the gym.

A GSOH is needed because rejection is inevitable, although not always personal.

Don't let a woman who rejects you make you act in an unflattering way. A relaxed guy who lets rejection roll of his sleeve will have way more fun.

If the relationship progresses to Level 2 dating, each person should be able to communicate openly and honestly with one another without hurting their partner.

There is a difference between a GSOH and funny. Women aren't attracted to guys who are always "on", instead they prefer to have them as friends.

There are health benefits to smiling and being lighthearted with a GSOH.

Your basic personality is not completely set in stone. If you were born a stick in the mud you can still adjust a little. You can be a nicer person.

Do activities to get yourself in a more playful mood like entertainers and comedians.

Humor feels good and you should keep a good story on hand like my dentist.

CHAPTER 8

LIKABILITY FACTOR 101

In order to be liked you have to make yourself someone worthy

- Aunt Rosa

MY CLIENT SHARED with me the story of when he was a boy of about eight years. He recalled coming home from school one day and the day was like most, rough.

He said his mood at home reflected his rough day as he was picking at his younger sister and also kicking and throwing things.

He said his mother was appalled at his behavior and had him take a time out and later asked "What is your problem?"

He said he told her, "Nobody likes me". And isn't that, usually, what the problem is in a nutshell? Every kid wants to be liked and it's no different when you reach adulthood, you still have that same core desire and the need to be liked.

This need to be liked tapped into my client's unfettered emotions (core human desires) and it was shutting down his rational mind and especially when he felt most vulnerable in dating situations.

My client is not alone in believing he is unlikeable, as that belief touches on two of five basic fears that all humans share to which all other fears are manufactured according to an article in *Psychology Today*.

The two fears are:

1. Separation. We're not enough.

2. Ego-death. We won't be loved.

Separation is the fear of abandonment, rejection. Feeling not wanted, respected or valued by anybody else. The "silent treatment," when imposed by a group (kids teasing), can lead to a devastating psychological effect. We are not enough. Or, "Nobody likes me," translates to we won't be loved and ego death.

At the end of the day all humans, all men operate off this fear and no matter how big you get, the little voice can still ring loud in your head, "Nobody likes me." This carries on to adulthood and dating. "Why would a beautiful girl like that want me?" "What if she doesn't like me?" These negative thoughts chip at your confidence.

This reminds me of a card that was tucked inside a plant my aunt sent to me in college. The card read, "In order to be loved, you have to make yourself someone worthy to be loved." Replace the word "loved" with "liked" and let's dive deep into Likability 101.

Take a minute and consider the characteristics associated with people who are likable (charismatic). You'll recall from the very first chapter that certain words like "charisma" means different things to different people.

Being likable or charismatic is not innate. If you aren't born with traits that naturally make you likable, which does not mean you can't build upon stuff that increases your likeability.

The list I'll share is "well worn", but most importantly it's "tried and true". Get it right and you are on your way to being a better more likable you.

BE TRUSTWORTHY & HONEST

Women do not like dishonest men. The dating apps and the so-called "dating gurus" have birthed a generation of liars. Those who float comfortably in the dishonest dating culture. The dating apps outsource real communication.

You can meet a lot of people in a short period of time and to juggle everybody there isn't time enough for authentic or real communication that takes place when you meet in person.

I cover my disdain for the dating apps in the *Digital Age Chapter* so I won't rehash it here, but just know that dating apps and websites make it easier to be deceptive.

You don't have to put up your real picture, or a current picture that shows how you really look. Even if it is a current picture, how many pictures did you have to take to get a flattering one?

Never mind that texting and tapping can never substitute genuine communication. It's a lot easier to tell tall tales to a tiny screen than it is to tell one to someone's face.

The so-called "dating gurus" don't make it any better. They may encourage in-person communication but it's groupthink and robotic. It's like a standardized test, say this and this and this and you pass.

The love gurus and dating schools might have good intentions, some anyway. The problem though is they teach the one size fits all model. Honey, when has one size ever fit all?

You are a smart man reading this book, so I don't have to tell you that being honest with a woman does not mean you give it all up on the first meeting or the first date.

Have some dignity why don't you? In seriousness, no matter how she makes you feel during the first meeting you don't and you shouldn't tell all on the first date.

There is a difference between being honest and telling all your business. It's easy to assume that women are the chatterboxes and tell all too soon but a man when he sees a thing of beauty can become weak and feel like he should propose on the spot.

Don't laugh, I know men who have proposed upon first meeting a woman and also made the foolish mistake of telling all of his business. If your ex-wife is trying to in your words, "take you for everything you have" why does this woman need to know that? If you will so easily dish all on someone you at some point loved, will you talk about her in the same way?

If your soon to be ex-wife cheated on you and brought you back some nasty disease even if you claim this was a long time ago and you are now cured, does this new lady really need to know that? You want to have a balanced disclosure. The way to build trust is to have a two-way conversation. Think back to John and Joan in the chapter on listening.

John listened to Joan and he didn't wait for her to finish speaking. He interrupted here and there. Having a two-way conversation with balanced disclosure is how you get to know another person. You can't possibly like someone you can't get to know.

Being someone considered trustworthy is not only about the words you speak from your mouth because you could be saying all the right things and or not say any of the wrong things, but your body language could be telling a different story.

A woman's superpower makes her very good at reading body language and she is reading you from head to toe and back up again. She's not only listening to what you were saying but the expression on your face when you said it. The body language will determine if she will like or trust you.

Alex Todorov a psychologist at the prestigious Princeton University says we can't help but form an immediate opinion of someone by their face.

According to Todorov we make up our minds after seeing a person's face for a fraction of a second and unless you are super good looking without even saying one word you have a few strikes against you. This does not mean you should throw in the towel. In fact, don't even worry about factors out of your control and instead focus on factors that are in your control.

You can control your facial and body expressions so that they exude honesty and trustworthiness. You can do this with things like looking a woman in her eyes and flashing a genuine "Duchenne" smile.

To avoid looking dishonest like that little boy "nobody likes" there are some movements to avoid. Don't fidget with your hands and don't cross your arms or legs which can suggest you are closed off, defensive, or not telling the truth.

Instead of closing off defensively, use open and engaging body gestures. This includes smiling, nodding and mirroring her behavior. You want the majority of the moves you make to be warm and inviting. Instead of overthinking every single move you make just remember these two words "Be Cool."

Be cognizant of your gestures, expressions and voice tones, which should be welcoming and inviting. Televangelist Joel Osteen in each sermon employs 9 of the 12 Charismatic Leadership Tactics (CLTs), every other minute. If the shy boy from Texas turned preacher man can charm millions, certainly you can charm a nice lady by engaging in an honest conversation that makes her feel special.

Don't Over Promise, Over Deliver

The Tinder apps have made a few men believe they don't have to do anything to get a woman and this is where any man willing to not only please, but over deliver, will have abundant success with a woman.

Let's say you have a date with a woman and you plan to cook her dinner. She asks if you are a good cook and you say "yes". Just a simple yes. Or maybe you tease a little bit, "I'm not too bad in the kitchen."

You say this knowing full well that you took a six-week cooking course in Italy and before that you were already an amazing cook. Not only do you make her a fabulous meal, you blow her away with a romantic backdrop.

She could have casually mentioned to you that she likes candles or dinner by the fireplace and although you acknowledge these things you didn't let in on the fact that you were taking some serious notes.

The dinner date goes amazingly well because you over-delivered.

BE LIKEABLE BUT NOT EASY

A woman likes a bit of a challenge. This means she likes to be admired but she does not want to be worshipped and especially not by someone that she has on the fence and is not yet sure if she wants to give you a chance.

Now before you revert back to the little boy who "nobody likes", her being unsure about you has nothing to do with whether or not she likes you. She may like you but perceive you to be a playboy and will pass you up instead of the risk of getting her feelings hurt.

Or she could be on the fence about you because of who you are. Maybe you have name recognition, money, or any of the other power traits that attract women.

She's not blaming you for your ability to attract women but she may need to see how you handle the attraction.

Do you string women along or do you let them down easily?

Another thing that might have her unsure about you is if you are too nice. Now this may seem silly but it really isn't. You see, women like a little challenge.

She doesn't want you tripping over her and doing everything without her even asking. Don't confuse "tripping over her" with being a nice guy. Women do like nice guys just not nice pets. Also, if a man comes across as too nice red flags appear.

That's because sometimes men are nice just because they want to sleep with a woman and that's all they want to do. After they get her in bed, they go back to being a not so nice guy.

I'm not saying that all men are jerks and I'm definitely not saying that you are one. But I'm sure you know of cases where men are really nice just to get women in bed and then they have no use for her.

DROP THE FAÇADE

Never try to be someone you are not. Women can detect BS and there are enough flakey people in the world. The façade could be making you out to be more than you really are.

I have a friend and he works in his cousin's business. Yet he's always taking credit as if he owns the company.

He's not the owner, he's the manager in the small company and a crucial reason why it's successful. Although he's the right-hand man and he occasionally runs things, he isn't running it.

Instead of putting on a façade and lying - there's an honest way for him to make himself look like a big shot.

That would be to acknowledge that his cousin owns the business and that he is the 2nd top guy in the business. Maybe he and the cousin have discussed obtaining some ownership or maybe he is studying so that one day he can have his own business. Being honest in this case demonstrates confidence in himself and shows he's honest.

When men try to pretend to be someone or something they are not they are usually hiding some insecurities. If not, they would be perfectly OK with saying I'm the office manager in the business, or I'm the assistant. It's better to be proud of who you are while striving to be better than to engage in falsehoods.

BE SPICY AND NEVER BORING

Thanks to the digital disruption and other things, women (and men) have a short attention span. To keep her interested you have to do something intriguing or interesting. This might be stepping out of your comfort zone and encouraging her to do the same thing. Instead of a regular date, plan something different interesting. Surprise her. Keep her guessing, wanting, begging.

BE ENTHUSIASTIC

If you are not in a good mood to be at a social gathering or on a date then don't come, or go home. This is similar to the example I used regarding having your phone out on a date. If a situation is that important that you must use or watch your phone, or be in a sour mood, then go take care of that situation.

Chances are whatever is causing you to be disconnected from your date and be in a bad mood is going to really eat you up when on top of that your date walks out unable to any longer deal with your sour mood.

If something has happened to dampen your mood and if going out isn't making you feel any better as you'd hoped, then go home and come back out when you feel better.

Sometimes, if it's not something major and it's something minor like you've had a tough day going out may help you shake the sour memories of that day. But if you don't think it can, or you've gone out and proven it can't, don't go or go home.

EMPATHY

The bottom line is likable people are empathetic people. Empathy allows you to step into the space of another person to understand why they feel the way they do. This is not about agreeing, it's about understanding as best you can. Empathetic people are likable because they give up some extra time that they could be doing for themselves or someone close to them and extend warm thoughts and kind words to someone in need. It could be a complete stranger.

Because of the 24/7 news cycle it appears heartless and cold-blooded people are everywhere. Empathetic people appear like a rare diamond.

It's not that they necessarily do something great, but instead they take the time to say a kind word or make a small gesture that shows they care. Women are turned on by an empathetic man.

BE HUMBLE, HAVE HUMILITY, BE HELPFUL

This is more than a catchphrase. You might be "the best" but so what if it's draped in a braggadocios attitude. If you do nice things and help people it is unbecoming if you brag.

Be the best and be humble about it. Have some humility. MMA and Boxing fighter Conor McGregor win, lose or draw shows humility at the appropriate time. Before the fight people trash talk, but after the fight both fighters are to be humble.

Do good on this earth. People who do good are likable.

They are more likely to contribute time or resources and they don't brag about the work they do. Women take notice of humble yet charitable men.

COMPLIMENTS

Women love compliments and paying a woman a compliment or some compliments aren't the same as falling all over her and being too nice. Women go out of their way to look nice for men and she enjoys it when you tell her she looks nice, or you say something nice about her. Again, there is a fine line between buttering a woman up and kissing her buttered up butt.

What traits would you like to have that you think would make you more likable? Quickly name 10 things. Below is my list. After reading my list quickly make your own list. It's OK to use stuff from my list and or to use more than one word.

1. Funny
2. Charitable
3. Hardworking
4. Good energy (exciting)
5. Easy going
6. Compassionate
7. Organized
8. Firm when needed (No one respects pushovers)

9. Interesting (plays Golf and Chess)

10. Relates well to young and old

If you are anything on this list you are likable. The next list fits traits of someone who is not likable.

1. Easy to anger

2. Loud

3. Conniving

4. Uncaring (never willing to help)

5. Disagreeable

6. Pushy

7. Creepy

8. Erratic (happy then mad as hell)

9. Over the top (boring)

10. Inappropriate

Your goal is to be more things on the first list and fewer things on the second list. Nobody wants to be the kid (or adult) that nobody likes. Take a breath however, because your desire to be likable should not turn you into a woman pleaser.

A woman who wants you to be things you are not or to enjoy the stuff you can't tolerate is not a good match for you. Be kind but most importantly to thine own self-be true.

KEY TAKEAWAYS

It starts as a kid "Nobody likes me."

It stems from two of five basic fears:

1. Separation. We're not enough

2. Ego-death. We won't be loved

Women do not like dishonest men. The dating apps and the so-called love gurus have birthed a generation of liars. Those who float comfortably in the digital underworld.

Here's the "well-worn" but "tried and true" list that makes you more likable:

Don't Over Promise, Over Deliver

Tell her you'll cook her dinner, but don't share that you have trained chef skills. Surprise her.

Be nice, but not easy

You want to be nice but you don't want to be a pushover.

Drop the facades

If you don't own the business but you are a crucial part of it, be happy with your success. Don't be a fake or a pretender.

Be spicy and not boring

What does it hurt to turn it up a notch or two?

Be enthusiastic

Enthusiasm begets good energy

Be Humble, helpful and have humility

Don't brag, just do.

Compliment her she'll love it, but don't overdo it

Don't kiss her buttered up ass.

Create a list of 10 qualities that make YOU an amazing catch.

CHAPTER 9

CHARISMA STYLE

Cause every girl crazy 'bout a sharp dressed man

- ZZ Top

ENTIRE TV SHOW storylines have revolved around a popular guy trying to help the unpopular guy get the girl. One way he tries to help him is by giving him fashion tips, because let's face it, clothes make the man.

I recall seeing a syndicated episode of the TV show the Brady Bunch in which the older sibling Greg tries to help his younger brother Peter get a date by giving him tips on what to wear.

The problem was Greg helped Peter dress in the type of clothes that "he" liked and which looked good on him. The type of clothes that looked good on Greg didn't look good on Peter and it made Peter feel stupid.

I might have the details of the episode jumbled. The point of the story is that your style should always make you feel comfortable and authentically you. If you don't feel good in the clothing you wear, you won't feel confident.

Stick with a style of clothing that makes you feel comfortable, but also be open to different choices. I advise that you keep an open mind and on occasion, try something new. I get it you are comfortable wearing what you always wear.

Probably the more you resist, the more you need fashion help. Are you stuck in a fashion phase of a time period from decades ago? Maybe on a casual day you throw on t-shirt and jeans, not the stylish kind. Do you enjoy the nerdy look, or perhaps you don't give a hoot about how you dress?

Although on occasion I'll encounter a client who completely misses the mark, most of the time and probably most of you reading this dress OK and don't need a major fashion overhaul, just a small fashion tweak.

Small improvements to how you dress can make all the difference in the world as to how you look and feel. Women will view you differently and your dating life will improve. Wearing what you always wear if it doesn't make you look and feel good, will get the results you've always gotten; a lackluster dating life.

WHY WHAT YOU WEAR MATTERS 101

Society puts more emphasis on women looking and dressing nicely which makes some men think they can slide comfortably under the fashion radar and this is simply not true. What a man wears matters to his dating life and confidence. The right kind of clothing helps you project charisma and look better.

Stop and consider how much of your body clothing covers. Depending on the season and what you are wearing, clothing can cover 90 % of your body. Let that percentage sink in for a minute. Once again Dr. Albert Mehrabian's communication percentages come into play.

7% relates to the importance of the words used

38% refers to voice tone and inflection

55% refers to the importance of face and body language

If you accept those percentages and most communication experts do, then half of the way you communicate is with body language and your body is usually draped in clothes. If your clothes are ill-fitted then your body language probably is too.

MOOD

How you look in your clothing sets your state of mind. You most likely won't operate the same in outdoor attire as you would in dating attire. When you take the time to dress nicely for a date it sets the mood.

Everything from showering, to grooming, to putting on nice clothing can put you in an exciting mood. You are taking the time to look good and it will shine through in your demeanor.

CONFIDENCE

The right fitting clothing helps you look better. For instance, there are confidence boosting benefits to wearing a fitted sports jacket. It helps you build your shoulders (maintain good posture), and adds height. It will trim a few pounds off your beer gut if you have one. Your midsection will look smaller and you will look taller and even more so if your jacket is buttoned.

EXCITEMENT

Update your wardrobe by adding a few new pieces, even if it's just a belt, tie or a pair of socks, and if you are in an especially daring mood, add a splash of color and invite even more excitement into your dating life.

When you get something new, it makes you feel happy. When you dress nice, you look and feel good and that draws good energy from women.

I will caution that you might not want to try something "too new" on a first date otherwise it might take you to far from your comfort zone and prevent you from feeling present in the moment.

WHERE TO GET FASHION ADVICE?

When men give other men styling tips it's usually from a collection of what they like and not what will look good on you. What Greg liked and what looked good on him, didn't work for his brother Peter.

It's best for men to take styling advice from a woman, and yes, I might be a little biased. A woman with even an ounce of fashion sense can tell what looks good on you. Let her roam through your closet or take her to the store with you when you go shopping.

If you don't have someone to go shopping with you can always check out the mannequins at the store. They usually have stylists who put together outfits on the mannequins so you can take advantage of their knowledge.

You can also seek help from salespeople but be leery of them if they work on commission as they'll probably tell you everything that your money can buy looks good on you.

This does not mean the salesperson is necessarily being dishonest and maybe she really thinks you look OK in the clothing. The problem is you don't know if they are being real with you or not.

As a personal coach I work with my clients to give them advice on clothes or I send them to a stylist since it's their job to know what looks good on you.

A stylist does not want to take you away from your style, she wants to bring you into it. Her job is to tell you the honest truth. A stylist can help you go through your current wardrobe and also find new stuff to wear. It's well worth the investment in yourself.

A stylist is your best option but if not within your budget proceed further and check out my fashion advice.

FASHION DOS & DON'TS

I don't know you personally so I can't give you personalized fashion tips. However, these general tips which are in no particular order can help you dress better.

DO. Spruce it up with a splash of color. You might prefer the basic colors that never go out of style. You know standard colors like, blue, black, tan and maybe grey. There is nothing wrong with the staple colors but every now and again try something different.

You don't have to start with your entire wardrobe, maybe you start by sprucing it up with a different tie, or a pair of socks or some great shoes.

DO. The ladies know if (and you should too), that if you have something in your closet and you haven't worn it in over a year, ditch it because you probably aren't going to wear it and there's a reason it's not one of your favorites.

There is some clothing that will stand the test of time and you can keep it a little longer or forever if it's sentimental, but if it has a moth smell to it you probably want to ditch it.

DON'T. Do baggy or tight. It's been fashionable to wear both baggy clothing and skin-tight clothing. However, unless you're a celebrity or have the personal cell number of a fashion icon, stay away from too loose or too tight clothing as a rule.

There are exceptions for certain body shapes. If the skinny

look fits you like a glove, the next time you go shopping you might try the next size down.

DO. It's OK to dress casually and wear a t-shirt and jeans as long they are up to date. No mom jeans please.

DO. Put on a good pair of shoes made with quality. My grand-mother had a saying. It goes like this, "If you have on a good pair of shoes and your hair is combed you could conquer the world." She lived during the depression, and granted things are slightly different now but it still holds true.

With shoes you need different kinds for different occasions. Nothing beats a good quality dress shoe, casual shoe, or sandal. While we are on sandals, don't ever wear socks with sandals and please don't wear white socks with dress shoes.

DO. If you are wearing a suit your footwear should match. Black suits need black shoes. Brown suits need brown shoes. There are a couple of wild cards, if you know fashion then you'll note that a navy suit can go with black, brown, camel, or oxblood col-ored shoes. Belts should match shoes.

DON'T. Running shoes are for running or while exercising. Never wear them beyond those areas. Some options are just as comfortable to wear out as your running shoes like casual sneakers or loafers.

DO. Groom Yourself. I'm sure you shower every day but you can't go wrong with showering before a date.

If you get off work take the time to hit the refresh button unless of course you go straight from work. If you are able to shower, be sure to switch out underwear and other pieces of cloth-ing in which sweat clings too.

I have a not so well-groomed client who is a rising entrepre-neur with a hot startup. At the moment he's busting his butt and raking in good money. You win in one way, you lose in others, and at the moment his dating life is losing. He came to me for help to figure out why.

I informed him his dating life is suffering because he stinks! Sure, he bathes and doesn't smell bad, but he has a stinky look. His business commands a lot of his time and when he does make time to go out and mingle it's as an afterthought with a last-minute invite from a few buddies, and he looks stinky.

He showers but does not wear cologne. He usually throws on a pair of shorts and flip-flops, which is fine except there's four days' worth of scruff, no haircut, long nose hair, and it's a stinky look.

The casual attire might work on occasion since he is just grabbing a few beers with the guys. The problem is where men grab beers, women grab wine.

He's a decent looking guy with a rapidly growing bank account and that makes him attractive. However, being poorly groomed is not sexy and certainly does not make one feel confident.

When you feel confident your body communicates confidence which attracts women. Grooming is the first and important tip to being more confident.

As women, if our hair is freshly styled, our makeup is great, our eyebrows and nails are beautiful, and our dress hugs our body in all the right places, we look and feel more attractive and our body radiates confidence. It's not different with men. When a man knows that he looks like a million bucks, he acts like it.

The excuse my client uses for having poor grooming habits is that his business keeps him busy. He says when he makes time to relax and chill out it's at the last minute. That's a load of bullshit. Even if he is busy and who isn't, take the time to cut your nose hair, shave your beard and get a haircut.

I interrupt this story to return to more fashion tips.

DO. Shave properly with a quality razor so you don't have a soul patch. Beards have more recently made a comeback.

If you are doing the beard thing be sure to keep it neat, clean and trimmed. There was a study recently that shared all the awful things that hide in beards. YIKES!

DO. Cut nose and ear hair.

DO. Dab on cologne but not too much.

DON'T. Don't Dress sloppy. You may be tempted to do so but never leave the house wearing a poor clothing choice regardless of where you are going.

With your career or business it might be protocol to dress a certain way. If in your job or career you must dress a certain way, then on the days you don't have to dress that way it might be tempting to throw on something comfy like a t-shirt and jeans.

Or maybe a t-shirt and jeans is your usual wear but you only save your good jeans and t-shirts for when you are going somewhere special.

If you are just going to say Home Depot to grab something you need for the house or out to grab a pizza you are probably tempted to put on "just running out of the house clothes". But single dateless guys shouldn't do this.

I'll let you in on the secret that most women won't even go to the gym without fixing themselves up a little and putting on a little make-up.

It's probably easier for you as a man to go out looking any old kind of way, but again if you are single go that extra effort to look dressed to impress even if it's just t-shirt and jeans, make sure you are wearing the nice ones and a nice pair of clean shoes.

DO USE THE OPPORTUNITY

Make a great first impression. I don't personally believe you get only one chance to make a great first impression because there are tons of cases where you meet someone and you aren't fully attracted to them but then something happens and they end up being attractive to you later.

I do however believe your first impression upon her first meeting you, or you first going on a date that you want to wow her.

You can wow her by being dressed to impress. If you are dressed impeccably and you are not on a date you will catch the ladies attention. If you are dressed impeccably and you are on a date you'll keep her attention.

DO. Look for best colors. Color can set the mood.

Red shows your passion and that you have energy. You want to wake her up, wear a splash of red.

Blue suggests trust. It's a reason why social media sites like Facebook or Twitter use the color blue. Some say the darker the blue, the deeper the trust. You want to connect with her wear the trust color.

Grey and tan are good neutral colors for anytime dating or otherwise. You want her to take you seriously wear the neutral colors.

Some colors like orange or yellow are flashy and flamboyant so unless you are a stylist stay away from them.

DEEP STYLING TIPS

Health and fitness as you've been told your entire life and elsewhere in this book are important to your fitness levels and how you look. You may never get a perfect body but you can get it more perfect than not.

A nice smile is so important. A long life of living, eating and drinking coffee might have run havoc in your mouth. If this is the case consider a deep cleaning, teeth repair, whitening and or replacement.

If you are going bald keep your hair cut, cut it off or do the miracle growth thing, hair plugs if you prefer.

Don't rule out doing anything to make yourself look and feel better.

I realize that some of the tips are not earth-shattering and also that men are generally either into fashion or they are not. I'll repeat, how you win in charisma and dating is by making overall improvements in each area of your life and this includes in fashion.

The bottom line is, you don't have to set the fashion world on fire but do improve your look to light a fire under your dating life.

KEY TAKEAWAYS

Your style should always make you feel comfortable and authentically you. However, don't be afraid to step out of your comfort zone and try something new.

Clothing can cover up to 90 % of your body. Over 50% of communication is with body language, draped in clothing.

Clothing conveys Mood, Confidence and Excitement among other things.

The best place to get fashion advice is from a personal stylist or coach. If that's not an option there are other options, such as from a woman, checking out a store mannequin, or a magazine.

There are fashion Dos and Don'ts. No nothing is ever set in stone, but some things you don't want to be caught dead doing/wearing.

How you look is directly related to how confident you feel so, by all means, do whatever you can to look better.

CHAPTER 10

CHARISMA IN THE DIGITAL AGE

We live in the digital world, but we're fairly analog creatures

- Omar Ahmad

IT'S A LITTLE hard to swallow that a 5.5 inch hard, rectangle shaped device gets more interest than she does. That's the message you are sending when you are constantly swiping your phone when you are out mingling and or dating.

When Dr. Albert Mehrabian's research was conducted over four decades ago and he gave the percentage breakdown of nonverbal, verbal and voice tone communications, there was no way to factor in digital communication which hadn't yet happened.

In today's world there's small talk, body talk, nonverbal talk and oh yeah, digital talk. The Digital Disruption.

What don't most of us do digitally these days? We work, we shop, we get entertainment, educated, help with boredom, help with keeping unwanted people away from us a term I call digital cockblocking.

You may not have heard of the phrase cockblocker before. If not, a cockblocker is a person who prevents you from talking to a girl for the purposes of hooking up, whether this is for a date or getting her in bed.

If this phrase doesn't ring a bell you may call it something else and as you'll see it's used in every situation from business to dating and beyond.

It isn't always that you want to be blocked because you don't like the person who wants to make contact with you and it could be for a variety of reasons.

When it comes to matchmaking, I like to meet women I screen in informal atmospheres so that it feels relaxed. We may appear to be a group of girlfriends hanging out but actually it's business.

I shared about my friend Jenny meeting Jack in the coffee shop. At first glance she didn't think Jack would be someone who'd interest her, not to mention her social anxiety kicked in so she began hyper-focusing on the book she was reading. In this case the book was the cockblocker, still Jack used the three-second rule and went for it.

Jenny's first response was to hand the book back. Jack's quick response was hand the book back with a note inside. His confidence and his great smile lead to a conversation and they are still together today. Moral of the story: Don't let the cockblocker (rouse or red herring) stop you.

Whatever your reason you can't be bothered and whatever you call it, if you can't or don't want to be bothered, you'll take action so you don't have to be.

You might do something like pretend to be reading a newspaper, or walk faster pretending to be in a hurry, or focusing on something you are doing like reading a book. You might even pretend to be using your cell phone which is a modern-day cockblocker.

In the digital age there's the phone as the cock blocker, and the "nerve easer".

Perhaps phones are to this generation what smoking was to the baby boomer's generation. My best friend's parents were chain smokers. They started smoking in their tender teens. I'm told back then smoking made you look cool, not be bored and deal with social anxiety around the opposite sex. Sound familiar?

My friend's mother would be quick to say she needed a cigarette to calm her nerves. I have had more than a client or two who are very confident charismatic businessmen tell me that they experience nervousness and or social anxiety when on a date and that a phone serves as a vice to calm the nerves. Translated, help them not be present.

Fear in social dating situations causes you to hang on to your phone as a nerve calmer or protective shield. I set my client up with a date and the woman shared with me that the entire time he was looking at his phone, nonstop swiping and tapping. She said he only occasionally looked up from his phone.

My client later told me he had a bout of anxiety come on all of a sudden. He said it happens to him and it did even more with this women because in person her beauty far exceeded her pictures. Social anxiety indeed shows up unexpectedly. That particular date actually ended in a marriage but it almost didn't because of the phone and fear.

A woman does not want to be on a date with you while you're doing tapping and swiping. If you are out looking to mingle or on a date, put your phone away otherwise it's just rude. Fidgeting with your phone comes across as nervousness with translates to no confidence.

In the case of my client he was not rude and instead suffers from social anxiety a common type of disorder suffered by 10% of the population according to the National Institute of Mental Health. If you suffer from severe anxiety you may need professional help, but in other cases there are things you can do to ease the nerves.

A person with social anxiety disorder feels symptoms of anxiety or fear in certain or all social situations, such as meeting new people and dating.

Some of the symptoms of social anxiety are panic, shame, fear of being perceived negatively, feeling embarrassed. The emotional symptoms can be accompanied by physical symptoms like sweating, blushing, rashes, dry mouth and heart racing. Whether you have emotional or physical symptoms they can come on without any warning.

Sometimes it's not social anxiety but nervousness that becomes a self-fulfilling prophecy. You tell yourself you are nervous, you start to believe you are nervous, you are nervous, because whether you believe it's true or not true, you are correct.

I'll cover things later in the chapter to ease nervousness and mild cases of social anxiety. For now just know that when you are out trying to meet women or if you are on a date, there is NEVER a reason to have your phone out or check it. If a situation is so critical that you have to be notified by phone, you should be there dealing with the situation and not on a date.

Even if you are expecting a call, what would happen if you were unavailable for one hour? One hour with your phone off will not ruin your business or cause you to lose your job, and if it does happen it's something more serious than one hour with your phone turned off that caused it.

Even if there is a family emergency, let's say your Dad is sick and may need to be hospitalized for the hundredth time or may die. What could you do for your Dad's situation immediately that you couldn't do in one hour? If your Dad 's situation is very important then go be there. Otherwise stay in the present moment minus your phone on.

I do not like getting phone calls or knocks on my door in the middle of the night because it scares the hell out of me. I have advised family, friends and staff that if something happens that I need to know about during those hours, save it until the morning since it's likely I can't do anything about it until then anyway.

You might be crying foul at advice to put your phone away because after all this is the digital age.

Everywhere you go whether it's a bar or (fill in the blank) social gathering, at work and even at sacred places people are tapping, swiping, texting, sexting, taking (pictures), or on some digital platform, hanging deep in the digital world and not the real one, which means they are not present, a key trait of charisma.

Since everyone is doing it you can stand out by not doing it. If you are at a social gathering instead of giving your undivided attention to a device, how about checking out the sights, sounds and scenery. It's called mindfulness or being present in the moment.

I was at a reception at a hotel and the artwork was amazing. So was the indoor water fountain, marble tile and I could go on and on. I enjoyed taking in the scenery and talking to people. There is so much to do and see when you are out and present in the moment.

If you meet a woman or are on a date and she sees you put away your phone, she will mirror your actions if she's interested in you. Or you could even go so far as to ask her to excuse you as you put away or turn off your phone. If she's interested she will surely follow.

Recently we had a lot of storms and hurricane weather in Punta Cana. I called to check on a friend after power was restored and he told me that he was fine and that everything including the lights had been out.

He stated he enjoyed the bonding with his girlfriend since they had no phone chargers or charged phones and it forced them to talk and focus solely on one another.

Have you ever been in the house with anyone and you never spoke just texted? It's sad when you think about it but I see people all the time out with friends not saying a word and instead texting away.

ON BECOMING LESS SOCIAL

With phones and electronic devices that contain what seems like everything you need to stay busy in the digital world, people are becoming less social, their social interaction skills are lacking and worst people are actually becoming anti-social.

A *Times* article shared that researchers from the University of Maryland's Robert H. Smith School of Business conducted a study in which participants were asked to use their phones doing various activities for a few minutes.

Another group of participants was asked to put their cell phones away. It's no surprise that the study participants who were allowed to use their phones demonstrated anti-social behavior. They were more likely to turn down volunteer opportunities or give money to charity. They also couldn't focus long enough to complete simple word problems.

Larry Rosen, a research psychologist who studied the impact of technology for over 30 years, on over 50,000 people from dozens of countries, including the U.S., concluded that (no surprise here) technology is a major game-changer in real relationships.

The research participants in Rosen's study were teens to adult participants. Rosen found the majority of smartphone users under the age of thirty-five years old, checked their electronic devices many times a day without any type of alert.

Stop right now and consider how many times you check your phone without any alert? Be honest, do you check your phone several times per hour, or more?

DATING APPS AND THE ART OF DEVALUE

There's body talk, small talk, and something Dr. Albert Mehrabin couldn't possibly have forecasted what was coming, digital talk in the form of dating apps, etc,.

I saw a picture in a magazine of a cartoon penis swiping a dating app on a cell phone. Be honest, what is on your mind when you hop on a dating app or find your way to a dating site?

You are looking for a hook-up more than you are expecting to find a high-quality woman to date seriously. There is no way really to find true love on those sites because they become tainted.

There are some things digital technology makes easier and there is some stuff it makes worse. It may make the art of hooking up easier, but it makes dating worse. Men say things to women after seeing their picture that they would never say to her in real life upon first meeting. "Wanna fuck?"

What is worse some women answer "Yes". This is according to those who f$@k-and-tell on dating forums and anonymously through magazine articles. The dating app and hooking up culture is the hot new thing that is quickly fading and will soon run its course.

Men play all kinds of games on the apps that they would never do in person. They put a picture up of a pet that they do not own. They only put one picture of themselves up in a group picture. They throw shady lines that they would never use in person. They use photos of people other than themselves or fake profiles to "cat-fish" or lure others into meeting them.

The dating apps and cheap bargain basement dating services might serve a certain purpose and or provide a type of short time satisfaction but it is certainly not the best dating and relationship option available.

For example, if you are a shy man who is afraid to approach women, hiding behind your phone app might give you a boost of digital courage, but your battery life will run out and eventually you'll have to come from behind the app and the broken sentence texts and meet her in person.

I get it, phones and electronics are powerful intellectual things, but as hard as they try they can't duplicate or replace authenticity which is the heart of charisma and meaningful relationships. Authentic communication in order to be authentic has to be based on in-person interaction.

If you are thumbing your nose up at digital babies because you are not digitally addicted then there may be other things that keep you from being fully present in the moment. Whether it's a phone, anxiety, or focusing on an issue that you can't change while out mingling or on your date.

Maybe you're the type of guy that reads the newspaper every day and that's what distracts you. The 24/7 news cycle will have you living on the edge of your seat. If it's bad news and you hear about it on the day of your date, it can affect your mood on a date even if the date is later in the evening.

Whatever the case the results are the same in that you may make the woman feel devalued.

If you do fall in the pool of the digitally addicted, you know better.

Whatever generation you are in you learned rules from parents and teachers. There is a reason you couldn't have on headphones at the dinner table or in class. You were taught the importance of interpersonal skills.

Eventually though, you'll crave real interaction and to have it you need interpersonal skills.

NERVES NOT OF STEEL (MANXIETY)

Nervousness and social anxiety are real and I want to share some tips that can help. But if you feel you suffer from severe anxiety please seek treatment. If you feel mild anxiety or nervousness there are things you can do to help you relax.

These are suggestions that have helped others but keep in mind there's not a one size fits all type of solution.

Let's start with me suggesting you get active, do some type of **physical activity** just before your date as a way to relax your nerves. Consider what you usually do before a date? You might catch a game on TV, you might run errands or who knows. I suggest you take a good old fashion walk and no, walking while doing errands does not count.

I have lots of friends that are involved in yoga, I prefer hot yoga because of its detox benefits. If you are already an active person you might switch up your routine and exercise an hour or two before your date.

You might try an app such as Insight Timer. Yes, I told you to put your phone away and now I'm asking you to take it out and listen to this meditation app before your date. Apps aren't bad, nor is technology. It only becomes a negative if you use technology at the wrong time or more often than not as it leads to poor or ineffective interpersonal skills.

Being nervous or feeling anxiety will cause you to focus on

what might go wrong on a date or after a date. It's the coulda, woulda, shoulda recording running in your brain. This loop of activity will make you feel helpless and maybe even dread your date. When you worry, your body produces stress hormones and nervousness is the opposite of relaxation. You'll find that a good medication app will help calm nerves.

You can relax by listening to and if you are really feeling full of yourself, dancing to upbeat music. You might be saying to yourself something like 'I listen to music all of the time', I bet you do, however consider if it's intentional. Be intentional about the music you listen to before a date so that it's the type of sounds that relax you.

Take deep breaths and practice breathing right before you go out. Don't turn your nose up at this tip unless before each and every date you try it. You might have heard of breathing exercises, but are you doing them right before your date?

Another tip is to jump in and face your fear because you can't conquer them if you don't face them. Think about jumping into a cold pool (or shower). It's going to be a cold dip but the cold quickly passes over to warmer temperatures. The more you go out jumping in pools (mingling or dating), the more confident you will feel.

There's no denying that technology like the cell phone or apps are not all bad and there are many benefits. But do not turn a blind eye or deft ear to the negative drawbacks of the digital disruption as it can make you a lazy ineffective communicator and turns some deceitful as they hide behind profiles.

In short, being aware of how electronics affects you as a person and also your dating life is crucial to you being successful at this thing called charisma and dating.

KEY TAKEAWAYS

Dr. Mehrabian couldn't have predicted the digital disruption. We do everything on our phones from shopping, working and seeking entertainment. We like to escape to the digital world.

The cell phone on the one hand has made our lives simpler and safer. They help cockblock, calm the nerves (Men sometimes have Manxiety). They also make you an ineffective communicator and less charitable.

Dating Apps devalue women. Nothing can replace real-life communication.

Put your phone away even though everyone else has their phone out. Be different and you'll stand out. If you put your phone away nothing important will happen that you can't fix when you turn your phone back on.

When your phone is put away you can be present in the moment and concentrate on being mindful.

Do something that helps you relax before a date. This can include: Exercise, Apps, Music, or anything that calms you.

CHAPTER 11

GET YOUR ACT TOGETHER

Cancel your pity party, pull yourself together and take total ownership for everything in your life

- Les Brown

YOU'VE BEEN SET up with the perfect woman. She looks to be everything you wanted and more and the good news is that she's just as attracted to you as you are to her.

The not so good news is women, just like men, aren't attracted to someone who does not have their life in order. On paper you have your act together, in real life, uh not so much. In person she's incredibly beautiful, but on paper her record is unstable.

Imagine you've met a woman whose issues far exceeds her attractiveness. She has "mommy" or "daddy" issues, drama from past relationships, she feels entitled, she wants constant validation, she's still trying to figure things out, she has no goals, etc. In short, she's a hot mess.

Now flip the script and let's point the finger at you. You've found your way to this book because you recognize your dating life could be better. Part of the reason your dating life isn't as exciting as you want it to be - could it be that you have issues?

If you want to have a more attractive dating life, you have to resolve your unresolved issues. You have to get your act together. This doesn't mean go from flawed to perfect because that takes time, but you do want to be in a good dating space to be seriously ready for what might come your way.

If Mia comes your way and she's everything you want in a woman and more, she won't stick around if you don't have your life together and neither will Claire, or any other high-quality woman.

It might be OK with you as long as she sticks around long enough to fulfill your immediate needs. Your immediate needs are first and foremost sexual. You might also need an escape from boredom, loneliness or a long work week.

This cycle of rinse and repeat dating is an immediate fix until it gets old and trust me on this one honey, date after date after date gets old eventually. Women's biological clocks tick and so do men's. Tick tock. Tick tock.

A lady will come along and sweep you off your feet. She will catch your heart in a way that you didn't think could happen. Guess what though? If you don't have your act together, when the wild, fun, partying and sex romps stop, the jokes going to be on you.

You'll tell (her name goes here) that you are ready to settle down and she'll look at you like you are crazy, not because she does not want to settle down, she does, just maybe not with you. This will hurt.

It goes back to prehistoric days that men are in charge of things and relationships and frankly many women like it that way. They easily let the man make the decision on if and when the relationship will move forward. There are cases however, when bells go off and red lights flash.

You'll recall, women have a superpower called women's intuition, which are the flashing bells and whistles that tell her that you are not the right guy for her to establish a committed relationship with.

She really enjoys you and your sex. You make her orgasm. Dating you is fun but she couldn't possibly see herself in a long-term relationship with you. She can't take you to meet her family and there's no way she can possibly meet you at the altar.

You buy her nice things, she does nice things for you and vice versa. That's all it is with you though, it is fun. You make her feel good on the surface. You are a good playmate and it's a playdate she very much enjoys.

Your ego may stroke you into believing that you are everything a woman could want in a man and that there's no way possible a woman could not want to settle down with you. You are a successful (fill in the blank). You own a (fill in the blank), you drive or sail a (fill in the blank).

Your ego tells you that you are good looking, in shape, well groomed, well dressed and you have many of the traits that make you appear successful on paper.

In this case the ego is not lying to you, you really do "have it going on", even though you aren't relationship material at this point. Your heart may tell you that you are ready but your actions reveal the truth, YOU DON'T HAVE YOUR ACT TOGETHER. There are telltale signs to support this.

As a matchmaker and relationship coach I have clients who come to me with honest intentions. They want to find a love connection with a woman. Initially all that I can go by is how impressive they look on paper and the information they choose to share.

I dig deeper to discover the essence of who they truly are because their happiness means everything to me. If they are happy,

I'm happy and successful. I offer premium services and integrity which is everything in this industry.

I'm open and honest with my clients when I tell them that just because they've been "set up", it's not a done deal. They believe if they show up for a date, looking good on paper, that's good enough to land the woman of their dreams.

While it is true that on paper they look fantastic. Their bank account and resume look fantastic. They have a good appearance and style. They don't lack charisma. They have good body language; the list is long and impressive.

This impressive list makes some clients believe that they don't need to resolve unresolved issues, or that they don't need to improve their social interaction skills.

They believe that because they have effective business skills and business relationships, this carries over to dating and interpersonal skills.

If you are effective in business you probably do have some solid social skills. Nevertheless, business is still a transaction. You (your company or employer) has a service or product and a client or customer pays you.

Being able to service a client does not mean you know how to make her feel special. Just because you know how to take care of a patient professionally does not mean you have patience.

I have a client who is a neonatologist. He is renowned and a top specialist in his field. He takes care of the smallest of human beings and I would certainly trust him with a newborn baby, but I wouldn't trust him to date my best friend.

He's used to being revered as the top in the world. His entire life since he was a kid he's been treated special and like the smartest person in the room.

He takes good care of babies, but not himself. He is wounded, carrying around baggage that he needs to dump somewhere. He needs to leave power and control out of a relationship.

Although I have a degree in psychology I'm not a psychologist, but my background as a certified coach working with clients around the world helps me to identify and offer up solutions for men.

Maybe you are like this client and you experience romantic apathy. You connect with someone pretty fast, it's mostly physical, and occasionally emotional. However, you get bored with them even faster. You don't like dogging women out but you can't stand being bored either.

You are attracted to beautiful women who you usually don't find interesting. The interesting women you don't find attractive.

Newsflash: The woman you find attractive and the one that you don't will eventually end up in the same average looking category. On the first day the attractive girl will be the most beautiful girl in the world. On the seventh day she'll be a nine, on the ninth day, she'll be a seven. On the twelfth day she'll be average looking and be in the same category in the looks department as the woman who you found to be unattractive or average.

The attractive girl and the average girl will both end up in the same boat. In other words, the newness and novelty will wear off from the attractive woman and all that will be left is your shared experience and things you have in common. If you have nothing in common, you'll develop romantic apathy. You'll get bored fast.

I'm not suggesting that you date women who don't excite you in the looks department, but if you are tired of getting bored so fast you'll want someone who shares or to which you can develop a common interest.

A way to fight through romantic apathy is to do introspection on a deeper level to determine what drives your attraction, unattraction, boredom.

You might discover that it really isn't that you have not found the right women, or that even if you found a woman you found attractive, who if at first took you emotionally and physically to the moon and back, it still would not work if you have unresolved issues. Even if the right woman landed on your lap she'd probably slip away due to your issues.

I have a male friend who I went to college with and our families are friends. Every time I see him he has a new girl on his arm introducing her as his wife or fiancée. I see the look of delight in the new woman's eyes because not only is my college friend good looking, he looks even better on paper.

I know the unresolved issues that my friend is working through and it's because of that reason I know that this current relationship like the one before that and the one before that can't possibly last. He knows it too and he's asked me, scratch that, he's pleaded with me to hook him up with the right girl.

He's a friend that I care about and would never take on as a client because he has deep rooted issues, stemming from his childhood and he needs to seek professional help first before I'll work with him to find a soul mate.

As I share with you the common issues that I see in men that keep them from enjoying the exciting dating life they deserve. If you have one or more of these issues that you can't resolve on your own after reading my advice, do seek professional help.

I've encountered men who resist professional help because of their pride, "Could something be wrong with me?" Well, yeah, but it doesn't mean the stuff can't be fixed and you can't be lovable, fuckable, dateable.

UNRESOLVED ISSUES

Daddy and Mommy issues. The way you grow up and the way you were treated by your parents can affect romantic relationships.

If you were neglected or abandoned by one or both parents you may initially cling to a partner because you have a fear of abandonment. Fear of being left alone or abandoned is a fear all men share. If this is your fear, you may be afraid of having a serious relationship or you might lose interest or exit relationships first if you fear she might leave you. You may want something permanent but fear of loss or rejection holds you back because of your childhood.

If your parent didn't make you feel good enough or loved, that is a form of abandonment. My friend growing up, his father wanted him to be good at sports and a boy's boy. His brothers were boy's boys in his father's eyes because they were good at sports.

My friend was a great intellectual then and still is now. Despite all he's achieved, he didn't feel loved by his father and he suffers from abandonment issues.

If as a child you were not made to feel loveable, capable or worthy, your fear of abandonment issues will carry over to relationships and you may feel a sort of "ego-death".

"Ego death" which is the fear of humiliation, shame or any other mechanism of profound self-disapproval that threatens the loss of integrity of the self. It is the fear of shattering or disintegration of one's constructed sense of lovability, capability, and worthiness.

This issue is something I believe my friend needs professional help to resolve. You may be able as an adult to resolve the issue with your parent. It could start with a talk, "Dad why did you make me feel so bad as a child?"

Maybe your Dad or parent had good intentions. "I didn't want you to be ridiculed, so I was tough on you."

If it's deeper than that, seek help.

UNRESOLVED PAST RELATIONSHIPS

You still have feelings for your ex-girlfriend, or she has feelings for you, or you have feelings for each other, or you like how she makes you feel in bed but you hate how she nags you. Whatever the case, you continue to take her calls because she's the go to one for sex when you are in-between dating situations, or you share a puppy together and you stay in touch about the puppy that you are parents too.

You both know it's really not about the puppy. She calls you to nag and tell you how you failed her in your relationship.

You know that the reason she's calling and the reason you keep picking up the phone is that she gives you the most amazing blow-jobs and every now and again when you are in between relation-ships, you need your cock sucked.

Therefore, you let her turn you on and off just like a faucet, even though at this present moment you are dating a

nice girl who does not nag you and makes you feel amazing in bed. You keep looking back because you've got abandonment or ego-death issues.

It's called a relationship mess or drama. If you don't let that relationship go you can't enjoy a new one.

Unsolved relationship mess could also tie back to the relation-ship that your parents had or have. If it is or was messy, messy may seem normal to you, although it is not.

In this case if you've got a family member or friend that you can share stuff with, they may be telling you what the problem is but you aren't listening. In the case of relationship drama, sometimes you don't need outside help, you just need to listen to your gut or a wise friend or family member.

YOU ARE ENTITLED

If you were the apple of your parent's eyes and they let you get away with everything and never said "no" to you, you may feel entitled. This could have carried on throughout your life, especially if you were good looking, smart, or had a talent.

Maybe everything was easy breezy for you growing up and you sailed perfectly into adult life where you did well with your studies. As an added bonus, your talent, intelligence, and or looks helped you find major success and power. You are at a point in your life where people don't dare challenge you.

This could present a problem in dating and relationships where challenges are a given. If you've never had to give and take you won't grasp that relationships have two halves. If you are entitled, she's entitled too and it's called reciprocity.

YOU WANT VALIDATION

You've come a long way baby. I previously shared with you about men who need validation. Making self-improvements isn't easy and you deserve a pat on the back. Here you go, did you feel that?

In dating and relationships if you need constant shots to the ego, you may not be as far along as you think.

A woman loves to praise her man because it makes her feel good too. She has no problem congratulating you on a business win, or telling you how attractive you look.

You are her man and it's an honor to make you feel good.

When making you feel good slips past compliments and into validation territory, there is an issue. A trait of a charismatic man is someone who projects warmth. How are you going to project warmth or compassion if you need frequent validation stamps?

If you constantly need validation, it could be because of your childhood, or some other reason. This can be fixed by stroking your own ego sometimes. You don't have to do it publicly. You stand in front of a mirror and tell yourself how good you look because of your self-improvements, whether that is a better diet, wardrobe, or any other improvement you've made.

You can take out a sheet of paper and write down your list of accomplishments beginning from where you started, to where you are now. The validation of yourself along with occasionally someone else doing it should be enough to keep the feel-good emotions going and if not, well you know what to do.

YOU WANT TO DO "X" BEFORE "Y"

"X" before "Y" simply means you want to do this before you start doing that. You might be busy building your career or your company. You might have a health issue, let's hope nothing major that you need to take care of before you can date.

You want to get to this fitness level before you start dating. You want to get out of debt before you start dating.

Things like the aforementioned means you need to do "X" before "Y". Maybe you can handle doing these things and dating, but if those things keep messing up your dating life. Go do "X" before "Y".

RELATIONSHIP GOALS

Not having relationship goals may not be unresolved issues exactly, but it is an issue that can affect your dating life.

Know what you want and not what you think you want. You think you want a serious relationship but your actions might reveal the opposite.

You think you'll settle down when you find the one. But when you find someone who meets the qualifications you excuse your way out of it.

Separate what you think you want from what you actually want. Take your dating life as serious as you do other things that are important to you, like your career.

With your career you get up on time, you take it seriously, you put energy into dotting your I's and crossing your T's. You make sure everything goes right and you don't play around with your career.

Whatever you've done the night before, when you go to work, you take it seriously. You know where you are now, where you want to be in five years and beyond. You are on target.

In your career it's very clear to see what you want in a specific way. You don't just say what you want, your actions speak too. You are taught your entire life to think about career goals.

When it comes to your love life you also should create goals, because goals without actions are just wishes. You may say something like "I want to get married and have kids." or "I want a long-term relationship" but have you cleared a path to accomplish such things?

With your career you may have cleared a path by going to school, working hard, gaining skills and it works the same way with a relationship. Do you treat your career differently than her or other important things you want out of life?

There is a saying" be careful what you ask for" and that is certainly true in dating. You have a good heart and good intention but now it's time to get real.

Are you ready for a relationship? Your mind or heart may answer yes, but what do your actions say? Are you just having a lot of fun dating and not ready for a relationship at this point? This could be because you are having too much fun or you have personal issues. Whatever the case, be upfront with yourself and the women you date.

Hugh Hefner died a playboy and I would think, a happy man. His relationship goals were to have multiple women and that's what he had, and the women agreed to that lifestyle.

Countless celebrities prefer the multiple women lifestyle and it works because they are honest about what they want. I don't want to pick on anyone, oh what the hell, I'll pick on Tiger Woods. He seems like a decent guy whose heart was in the right place.

He desired marriage and kids, but his man heart enjoyed sexual romps with babes. His reported infidelities hurt his family, as well as his golf game. This could have been avoided - maybe - if he approached or started from a place of honesty.

Honestly Consider:

Do you need to work on self-improvement before starting a relationship?

Is what you want out of a relationship about you or your desire not to hurt someone?

Is the reason you want to improve about you or the other person?

Are your dating goals specific enough, realistic enough? Do they feel like punishment or take you off focus?

Can you work through dating/relationship issues on your own or do you need help? I shared with you about my client who could take care of the smallest human being but not himself.

Women are flawed and men are too. You don't need to be

perfect to be dateable, but you'll fair better if you start from an honest place.

A woman will work with your flaws. After all she's human and you are too, but she might not stick around or want to take the relationship to the next level if you don't have your act together.

If you want to have an exciting dating life that is drama free, take a look at the man in the mirror. If you don't like what you see, fix it or seek help.

KEY TAKEAWAYS

Women like men who have their life together on paper and in real life. You don't just want to look good on paper, you want to look good in real life. Whether you have power attributes or you don't, you'll fare well in the dating department if you resolve unresolved issues first:

Daddy and mommy issues

If mom or Dad messed you up that bad, seek counseling.

Drama mess from past relationships

You like the sex which is why you keep your ex on standby, despite the fact that she's full of drama.

You feel entitled

Growing up you didn't get told "no".

You want validation

Look at me, I'm better than before.

You want "X" before "Y"

I want to make "X" amount of money before I get serious.

You have business goals only

You treat your business like a business, you treat dating like a hobby.

Some stuff is easy to fix, and sometimes you can do this by talking it out with a friend or the person that caused you to have hurt feelings. If your issues run deeper than talking it out, do seek professional help.

If you get romantic apathy or get bored, it's time to define your relationship goals.

CHAPTER 12

HOLISTIC CHARISMA

Life cannot subsist in society but by reciprocal concessions

- Samuel Johnson

THE YEAR WAS 1999. A young man with dark curly hair who looked like he'd been dipped in the fountain of youth, accepted the call. After repeatedly being asked by his father to stand in his shoes and preach at his 5,000-member church, he agreed.

The fire and brimstone preacher watched his son preach his first sermon from his hospital bed. One week later the father would be dead and the son had big pastoral shoes to fill. Within a year the son grew the church from 5,000 to 25,000 members.

Meet televangelist Joel Osteen who has been called the most charismatic man on earth. Each week thousands of souls flock to multiple services at Lakewood Church in Houston, Texas, and millions more listen to the inspirational messages or watch the preacher's son on television.

What does Pastor Osteen have that attracts about 50, 000 people and millions of followers in over 100 countries to his services? What does he have that makes so many people like and trust him? He's got a charismatic presence dipped in warm captivating sermons that make a large group of people feel good about themselves. Say it with me, they feel "gud".

Charisma has two halves. The relationship between the person who has it and the people (in Osteen's case the churchgoers), who respond to it. Charisma is making people feel good in general.

Let's leave the church house for a minute and focus on men, women, and dating. When a man spots an attractive woman, she's already started doing her part to make him feel good.

I know you are nodding your head and agreeing with this because science supports it. The researchers at the University of California found just being in the presence of a pretty woman causes temporary boosts in levels of testosterone and cortisol, the hormones associated with alertness and well-being in men.

The researchers found that just a five-minute talk with attractive women raised both the levels of the anti-stress hormone significantly. A woman knows what she is doing when she's taken the time to look great and she wants you to take notice.

She'd love it if you'd make her feel a certain way, whether you are just meeting her, or been on a few dates. You first take notice with your eyes and maybe a delighted smile. *Man, she's gorgeous.*

Next, compliment her with words. Not because she's conceited or ego-tripping, but because a part of her feels insecure. Wanting a compliment is not the same as needing validation and ego-tripping.

A woman wants you to take notice of her appearance since she did it for you. If she's single, she'll enjoy genuine compliments from men. If dating, she wants a compliment from her man.

It also wouldn't hurt if you gave her frequent compliments without overdoing it. Men can get away with being unattractive or out of shape far easier than women. If a woman is unattractive or even average looking, it puts the weight of the world on her high heels.

If she's gained a few pounds it can feel like the end of the world as she will be judged more harshly by both women and men. You might not have known her when she was five pounds lighter or before she had the nose or breast job. She may still see herself as a chubby, flat chested girl with the crooked nose.

Whereas you see her as a thing of beauty, she does not see herself that way and needs compliments. Don't confuse her need for compliments with ego. It's not ego, it's insecurity.

When you compliment her be specific and not generic. An example of a generic compliment is "you look fine."

What is "you look fine" really saying? Is it saying she looks better than a water buffalo? I mean really be specific. Don't say she looks fine, which is essentially saying that she looks average.

A generic comment might have been OK before her 25 grand worth of plastic surgery. Use exciting words when you compliment her, something like, "You look so amazing."

You aren't stroking her ego, she does not have one and you aren't lying. If you say she looks amazing and you mean her breasts, that's not lying.

Be careful though. There's a fine line between a compliment and kissing up, which women hate because it comes off as inauthentic bullshit. When you butter up a woman just dripping with compliments, fawning all over her, that is not sexy.

And whatever you do, please, please don't take her for granted if she does something nice for you, but you don't like whatever nice thing she does, still be genuine. Let's pretend she brings you a couple of soccer passes and plans to take you to the game for your next date. The only problem is you haaaaate soccer. Thank her for thinking of you and don't tell her right then that you hate soccer. Just accept the gift and be appreciative.

I'm not saying you have to make a big deal about the tickets and kiss her pedicured toes, but do acknowledge the action with gratitude, or in the future she might think twice before doing it again. You might be thinking right now *what about me, what about my needs?*

You are a smart man. Charisma is a two-way street of reciprocation, how you make her feel and how she makes you feel. Women have insecurities just like men. In the *Get Your Act Together* chapter, I tell men about your issues and insecurities but women are pretty imperfect creatures too.

She's got childhood issues, career issues, or *I'm not as attractive as my sister or friend* issues and she brings it to the table. If she lays too much of it on the table and she's a wreck, you'll know if it's the right situation for you or not.

If the little dings and imperfections are small and you'd like to get to know her better and at the very least have a one-night stand, talk her through her insecurities. I'm not asking you to be Dr. Phil but do show compassion and empathy, more traits of the charismatic man.

Be sure to make her feel good in the bedroom. Be a damn animal. I call it charismatic sex. Don't pull her hair and punish her unless she wants it, but don't hold back. With animal sex you don't hold back, even an animal knows that, although he has to conquer his prey. Unlike an animal however, there needs to be some comfort and nurturing as well.

Get your satisfaction but also pleasure her instead of rolling over and falling asleep. She wants good sex just like you, with some extra intimacy and foreplay. Holistic charisma is being tuned in and listening to everything, including her body. She wants kisses and hugs and foreplay and for you not to be afraid to get intense because she'll love it.

Don't treat her like a groupie and be insulting by placing her into generic female categories. For example: she's attractive so she has an attitude. Beautiful women are stuck up. She has this particular hair color so she's wild and dingy.

She has on expensive clothes so she just wants to spend my money. She's always talking on the phone to her girlfriends so she likes to gossip. If men are on the phone it's business, but women are gossiping. Get to know her in details and not specifications.

Let's recap some the things you must do to make a woman feel good about herself.

Compliment her with words and not just body language. Compliment her frequently, but don't butter her up and go overboard so that you appear foolish, strike a nice balance.

Don't take her for granted when she does something nice for you. Even if her niceness was a misstep, don't make her feel bad because she tried. You don't want to come off as uncaring and have her walking on eggs shells, hesitant to do anything else nice for you.

Help her through her insecurities because society rides women harder who don't have the right looks.

Love her good in the bedroom. Make her feel good, it's not just about you.

Pay her specific compliments. You don't buy generic stuff in the store because you know it's not as good as a name brand. She is not some generic chic, so don't put her in a generic or groupie category.

As we head on back to the church house let me be clear, I'm sharing information about Osteen because he presents a perfect example of holistic charisma to the world.

Whether you believe in God, science, or some other higher being or no higher being, that's perfectly fine. If you think he's unholy or a high roller, it doesn't really matter. All that matters is what you can learn from him about charisma.

Osteen's got a **win-win formula** in the church that you can take anywhere, including the Bunny Ranch to mingle with women.

The good thing about a formula is you don't have to do the hard task of reinventing the wheel, instead you ride the wheel and tweak as needed so that it fits your personal style to increase your charisma and spice up your dating life.

Osteen employs five tactics that produce a win-win formula that you can use in your dating life, but be sure to tweak it to fit your authentic style.

Tactic #1. Use other women to make you appealing to other women.

Osteen's members and followers watch a video or live stream before the sermon with a picture of Osteen's beautiful wife, the only person more beautiful than her is him.

At social gatherings men are seen as more attractive if they are accompanied by beautiful women. The women or woman could be a friend or someone they are involved with. This strategy works in the church house too.

Tactic #2. Make her think you only have eyes for her and say her name.

Osteen smiles warmly as he makes eye contact directly into the camera and although his messages are going out to millions of people, it appears that he is talking directly to you. Another charismatic trait is to directly address people by their name.

Tactic #3. Vocal Tones. Men, you don't want to come off as weak or lacking confidence, or worse, like you swallowed a helium balloon.

A big part of the delightfulness of an Osteen message is his vocal power and tone. His tone is very measured. He speaks slowly and not too loud, although he adjusts the volume when he needs to. He uses the emotional range of his voice to take you on a journey with him as he expresses hope, joy and all kinds of pleasantries.

Tactic #4. Humorous Story

Osteen opens his sermons with a humorous, what I'll call a story-joke, or a story that has a joke, which warms up the church. A big part of becoming charismatic is coming across as humorous and lighthearted, while being authentic. In meeting a woman or while on a date, a good sense of humor works every time.

Tactic #5. Verbal body language matters.

When Osteen is speaking, he commands the stage and uses appealing body language using his open arms to give the audience a big hug.

It doesn't hurt that Osteen appears wrapped in a complete charisma package. Osteen employs many of what charisma researcher John Antonakis, calls Charismatic Leadership Tactics (CLT).

One study concluded that Osteen uses 9 of the 12 CLTs every two sentences.

The 12 CLTs are:

1) Metaphors, similes, analogies

Osteen might say, "When you are following Jesus you are soaring like an eagle. You won't find an eagle stooping low, pecking in the chicken coop." You might tell her "Your smile is as inviting as a warm summer day."

2) Use contrasts and comparisons

Osteen might say, "The sinner and the saved, both need Jesus at all times."

You might say, "The promiscuous and the reserved both enjoy sex."

3) Ask Rhetorical questions

Osteen might ask, "Do you want to go to heaven?"

You might say, "Do you want to go to my place?"

4) Use a List, some say a 3-part list or phases. People remember things in threes.

Osteen might say, "Jesus, Lord, and Savior."

You might say,

If she's taller than you, she's not out of your league.

If she's the heir to the richest family in the world, she's not out of your league.

If the plastic surgery she's had makes her better looking than 90% of the women you know, she's not out of your league.

5) Expressions, Integrity and moral convictions

It comes across that Osteen sincerely believes what he believes and has integrity. Whether it's in the pulpit or at the bar stool you want to come across as authentic, i.e. having integrity and morals.

6) Reflections and Sentiments

Osteen might say, "Looking back before I was saved…."

You might say, "Looking back before I was single…"

7) Set high goals and ambitions

When Osteen asks his church to follow what the Bible says he's asking them to set goals.

Whether you are in pursuit of high-quality women, or making more money, you should set goals and be ambitious.

8) Project Confidence

Osteen projects confidence on the stage. You project confidence when you go out mingling.

9) Animated voice

Vocal Tones are key. Be conscious of how you sound.

10) Repetitions

Osteen might say, "The Saved, the Lost, and The Seeking."

If she's taller than you, she's not out of your league.

If she's the heir to the richest family in the world, she's not out of your league.

If the plastic surgery she's had makes her better looking than 90% of the women you know, she's not out of your league.

11) Facial expressions and gestures

Osteen's facial expression portrays happiness. His gestures with his arms and hands are open which translates to everyone is welcome, or everyone is invited.

12) Tell stories and anecdotes

Perhaps Osteen's most POWERFUL CHARISMATIC charm from my perspective is how he makes others feel using his influential storytelling abilities.

Before delivering a charismatic sermon, Osteen opens with a light-hearted funny little story with a message. His presence on stage is a steady stream of warm energy that could be seen as being shot with a dose of oxytocin directly to the brain.

According to researcher **Paul J. Zak** stories shape our brain and causes our brain to release oxytocin, the feel good chemical that flows through our brains limbic system, that can inspire us to do good things like volunteer or donate to a social cause, as well as change our attitudes and behavior.

According to Zak, "Oxytocin is produced when we trust someone or we are shown kindness."

Zak says stories that are emotionally engaging and compelling are better remembered.

Osteen's stories shoot the cuddle hormone (nickname for oxytocin) into his audience's veins and the dose makes them feel good about themselves and life in general and that my dear reader is charisma in a nutshell.

As you see, stories are a powerful force in shaping human behavior and they are instruments of connection. That's why as a relationship and charisma coach, one of the first questions I ask my clients is what's your story? Everyone has a story and should have stories in their go-to kit to make their dating life interesting. Stories are way more interesting than simply stating facts.

To tell your story you have to have a strong awareness of who you are. You have to be self-aware. Being self-aware means you know yourself intimately and you have a deep understanding of you. You are aware of the things that have brought you to the present moment and shaped you, your beliefs, emotions and reactions to your life experiences.

You must know who you are before you can get to know or connect with her.

Men who are self-aware tend to project warmth and most importantly have an emotional intelligence that allows them to have successful relationships. Before the words "emotional intelligence" became more mainstream you'd hear people say, "He just does not have common sense". Everyone knows at least one man and maybe even women who do not appear to have any common sense, aka emotional intelligence.

One study that measured the emotional intelligence quotient EQ found that it's more important than the intelligence quotient (IQ). You don't have to be Albert Einstein smart, but use common sense. Having a strong emotional intelligence factors into the holistic charisma formula.

You are self-aware, you have more than an ounce of common sense and now it's time to write your story. Pretend you are writing your story to give to a matchmaker such as myself, or to put your profile in my database.

How would you explain who you are? Take out a piece of paper and write out this information. So you don't feel overwhelmed, the paper could be a small index card or you could even speak your story into a smartphone. This is your chance to shine.

What's your story?

Keep in mind a big reason people fail at things like boosting their charisma or spicing up their dating life, is that they do not take action. They learn what to do, but then they don't do it. Don't be that guy who does not use common sense.

As an emotionally intelligent man who reads, take the time to do this exercise as it will help you discover who you are and help you become more datable.

This personal resume, although I've asked you to write it as if you are sharing it with me, is for your eyes only and to help you become more self-aware and improve your dating life.

Here are some things to include on your personal resume.

Your personality: Are you outgoing or not? Extrovert, introvert, ambivert or shy.

What are you like as a person, give some personality traits. Are you analytical or creative?

Your hobbies, what do you like to do and where do you like to do it, indoors or outdoors? If you have unique hobbies, what are they?

What is your job, career, or life like? Share this, as it shows your ambition. Women are attracted to ambitious men. If you don't yet have it going on, write about having it going on and things you want to accomplish which shows you're ambitious.

What are you looking for in a partner? Describe your ideal woman. Is she attractive? Does she have a sense of humor? Does she enjoy certain activities or hobbies? Is she a romantic? Write it down.

A side note, men usually have an easy list of what they are looking for in a partner. They want an attractive woman, sex, and food. Your easy list is OK but also go deeper, what other things really matter to you in a woman?

Women usually have the long list; loyalty, money, super sex, the stars, the moon and universe.

In creating your list, you are sharing your story. You don't have to be a magical storyteller to tell your story. Just be honest and authentic. Since the purpose of this exercise is not to share with anyone other than a person who may be helping you craft it, it's OK to include things that you are striving to be.

For instance, if you desire to be more physically fit, include that. If you are looking to lighten up and go with the flow more often, say that too. In addition to crafting your personal story, become a storyteller as it is a great way to connect with others.

You can share stories about your childhood, past or current situation, or your career and/or your passions.

If you tell your story through a recording, that will give you an opportunity to practice vocal tones which is key to telling a great story.

Osteen has complete command of his voice levels. His voice arouses and soothes. He's not known to speak in a loud tone but will raise his pitch as needed. He speaks to 50 thousand people in his audience and millions around the world, yet his followers - each and every one of them - think he is speaking directly to them. That's power.

TELL EXCITING STORIES

No one, not even you, likes a boring story. Make your story exciting. If you are talking into a device to share your story, do so in an animated way.

Read story # 1 and story #2. Which story do you think Joel Osteen would tell about Noah, from the Bible?

Story #1 Noah learned from God there was going to be a flood. He had seven days to gather up two of each of the animals. Exhausted from gathering up the animals, he drank some wine and fell asleep in the tent. His sons found him sleeping.

Story #2 Noah was a capable alcoholic who God called upon to save two of every species before the great floods. God can use anybody, even someone who fancies a little wine like Noah. He decided to drink himself unconscious after the great flood and fell asleep butt naked in the tent where his sons found him laying backwards across his bed like a car going the wrong way on a one-way street.

Osteen might not say butt naked but he would use engaging storytelling. When you tell a story you want to entertain, captivate and be ready to improvise.

When you entertain it means your date is going in a good direction. When you captivate it means your date is going in a great direction. When you are able to improvise, it means you've mastered charismatic storytelling.

A good storyteller uses metaphors, adjectives, and if appropriate, colorful language to tell a good story. A true test of authentic charisma is how you make others feel through verbal and nonverbal communication.

When Osteen started preaching he did so copying his father's fire and brimstone style. He quickly realized that was not his style and he morphed into a laid back authentic style that works for him. Lesson learned, you can't make others feel good if you don't.

AGREE TO DISAGREE

Using emotional intelligence (or common sense) means you know whom to share what with. Don't discuss stuff that causes you to start an argument or be disagreeable. Don't ever assume that you know what a woman's sensibilities are. Some topics are better left on the cutting room floor until you get to know someone better and even then, you might want to agree to disagree.

It's OK, and in fact it's advisable, that you be open and honest but never let your opinion lead to an argument. Couples that have been married for a very long time will tell you the reason that their love is lasting is because they can agree to disagree and that everything does not have to be an argument.

If men and women don't agree, agree to disagree. Don't get caught up in he said, she said, I think, she thinks stuff.

Here are some generalities that I found percolating in digital space as the differences between men and women. They are generalities indeed, with a tad bit of truth mixed in.

Women like to talk about people and relationships.

Men like sports and business.

Men talk to give information.

Women talk to collect information.

Men want power. Women want relationships.

Men focus on facts. Women focus on feelings.

Men like rules and structure. Women like freedom, fun and creativity.

Men want to think and women want to feel.

Some of the above is a generalization but some of it is because men and women's brains are wired differently and cross-communication can lead to disagreements.

A SPARK THAT IGNITES A FLAME

Use your spark to light her up and be sure to SAY HER NAME. Everyone loves hearing their name called. But don't overdo it. Say something like *Samantha, I want to share this (your story) with you.*

Men you are the spark in this book because the goal of the book is to help you to become more charismatic and have an exciting dating life. Which is why I refer to you as the spark and where your love life goes from here falls on your shoulders. Ignite.

The woman that you'd like to get to know or date has brought what she has to the table for right now. In the beginning what she brought is her attractiveness. Maybe it's the way she looks, her body, her smile, or something has set you on fire. Spark it and keep it going. Use your personal magnetism and allure to ignite her interest.

The two-fold of charisma is dependent upon how you present yourself and how you make her feel, which is why you want to present yourself in a good way and tell an interesting story about yourself and it will spread like wildfire.

What does that mean? Let's say you are single and want to date a woman. You may not have to go out searching and instead women will come to you. When you project "it", women will check you out and you won't know it until she sends a friend, sister or daughter your way. If she's not single she'll do her best to hook you up because you seem "different" than other guys.

I packed a lot into this chapter so don't worry if you can't remember everything that I share and if it all does not click in your mind immediately.

Remember your first day at your first job as a teenager. You were probably bombarded with too much information to learn for one hamburger shop that paid minimum wage. Every little detail does not have to stick immediately, but it will click.

I'll leave you with this, a good woman is not selfish, that is, if you make her feel good and she's interested she will also make you feel good. A holistic form of charisma is also about reciprocity. Give and get, live, love and receive.

KEY TAKEAWAYS

Charisma has two halves. The relationship between the person who has it and the people (in Osteen's case the churchgoers), who respond to it. Charisma is making people feel good in general.

A man's testosterone and cortisol level increase when they see a pretty woman.

You can make women feel good by:

Complimenting her with words and not just body language.

Doing so frequently, but don't go overboard and be seen as kissing up.

Don't take her for granted. If she does something nice, thank her even if she got it wrong.

Help her through her insecurities, society is harder on women's looks then men's looks.

Be good to her in the bedroom and make sure she's satisfied.

Don't make generic comments instead make specific ones.

You don't have to believe in God, science, a higher being, no higher being, be holy, unholy or even like or know of Osteen to learn from him and the charismatic win-win formula.

A study concluded that Osteen uses 9 of the 12 CLTs every two sentences.

The 12 CLTs are:

1. Metaphors, similes, analogies
2. Use contrasts and comparisons
3. Ask Rhetorical questions
4. Use a List, some say a 3-part list or phrases. People remember things in threes.
5. Expressions, integrity and moral convictions
6. Reflections and Sentiments
7. Set high goals and ambitions
8. Project Confidence
9. Animated voice
10. Repetitions
11. Facial expressions and gestures
12. Tell stories and anecdotes

John Antonakis who researched Charismatic Leadership Tactics says, "anyone trained in CLTs can become more influential, trustworthy, leaderlike and likable."

Osteen's best CLT is his storytelling abilities.

Paul J. Zak who founded the Center for Neuroeconomics states that oxytocin is important to storytelling (which Osteen masters) because stories have the power to change our behaviors and make us feel better. When you hear a good story consider how it makes you feel.

Write out the story of your life. Include things like; likes & dislikes, passion, hobbies or career goals. This information is for your eyes only.

Agree to Disagree with a woman but don't argue. Don't assume you know her sensibilities or that she knows yours.

CHAPTER 13

SILENCE YOUR INNER CRITIC

There is nothing either good or bad, but thinking makes it so

\- William Shakespeare

ONE OF MY clients had a speech impediment growing up and because of the way he talked he came across as a shy and awkward man.

He said he wasn't any of those things but because in his words he "talked funny", kids teased him and so he went through school and college without saying much and he didn't do well socially or academically.

He never dated in high school and only had one date in college.

He shared that when he was called on in class, although he usually knew the answer, he would sit there like a deer in head-lights or mumble a few words that no one could hear.

He didn't want his words to be audible because when people heard him talk he always got teased. The irony of it is he was teased for speaking and mumbling.

There were times he could have gotten a lot further, faster if he had confidence in his ability to communicate. He was asked to be the assistant editor of the school newspaper because he was a brilliant student with excellent written communication skills.

He didn't take the position because it would have meant more spoken communication and more interaction with people and more discomfort because of his speech. He thanked the editor for trying to give him a shot and he regrets now that he let his inner critic talk him out of a coveted position that was practically going to be handed to him.

People assumed he was awkward and now he looks back and concedes that the only thing awkward was his way of thinking. He said one time he walked in on a conversation where a girl he had a crush on was telling everyone that he was creepy.

He said what made the situation worse is usually when you bust someone speaking badly about you behind your back, they will become embarrassed and will apologize, at least that's the way he'd seen it go down on TV. But he said this mean girl doubled down with her insults when he walked in on the conversation. To add to her insults others joined in.

He said he would watch people in places like the library or cafeteria, not because he was "creepy" but because he yearned to join in on the conversation. He recalled that the people with the mean girl shared the exact places where they'd encountered him watching them too.

He got married and his first marriage fell apart and his inner critic blamed it on his lack of communication skills. Whenever there were challenges in his marriage and he wanted to communicate he became excited, which made him stutter, which made him feel self-conscious.

His less than perfect communication skills had been something that had been thrown in his face on occasion when he argued with his wife. Instead of arguing and sounding like an idiot, he did the opposite and did not communicate when there were challenges in the marriage.

In his early twenties he started his first business with a partner. He and his partner were young, they didn't really know what they were doing and the business didn't succeed. My client blamed himself because when he and his partner had a disagreement his business partner blamed the failing business on him not being able to make sales calls.

He made sales calls that usually didn't result in a deal because halfway through the conversation (if not sooner), he became nervous and began to stutter and this made the person on the other line either not believe him or hang up on him.

Psychologist Robert Firestone, an expert on all matters concerning a critical inner voice or what is often referred to as a silent inner critic, concluded that the critical inner voice is formed out of painful early life experiences in which we witnessed or experienced hurtful attitudes toward us. My client's classmates, wife and former business partner were hurtful to him in his early years.

Dr. Firestone says as a person grows up they consciously adopt and integrate a pattern of destructive thoughts when they fail to separate from their inner critic and they allow it to shape the direction of their lives, thereby vouching for the inner adversary, and sabotaging areas of their lives, including relationships.

My client in childhood "talked funny" and classmates viewed him as weird or awkward which in today's times might be viewed as him suffering from shyness or social anxiety. He internalized their beliefs and it affected the quality of his childhood where he was bullied and teased.

In his early 20's it affected his marriage and business. According to his inner critic those past things meant that he was an inarticulate failure. If only he communicated to his wife better his marriage would not have failed. If only he could speak better, sound more persuasive, he could have drummed up more business sales. Day in and day out his inner critic ran this stuff through his mind.

WHY IS YOUR INNER CRITIC SO DAMN NASTY?

To understand the nastiness you have to understand who is your inner critic and why does it attack you. Your inner critic is you and of course you know that; however, when you are being attacked by your inner critic it's hard to connect the dots that your inner critic is you.

Your inner critic pounces on your self-esteem and distorts how you see yourself and exaggerates how others see you. Even if a few idiots don't like you, you have to like you.

If you don't see yourself favorably it will show through your nonverbal body language communication. You will appear awkward, weird, creepy and your dating life will suck.

Your inner critic's (your) thought process is a faulty cycle like those old washing machines. The cycle begins with you believing it's true because you are telling yourself it's true. Because whether you believe it's true or you don't believe it's true, you are correct. Your inner critic is you telling exaggerated truths and it's up to you to believe it or not.

The inner critic is so damn nasty because regarding matters of being likable and dateable it believes as your risk-management dating advisor, a self-appointed title; it's saving you from hurt and rejection because rejection is painful and according to at least one study it feels like a punch in the gut.

Your inner critic wants you to be happy and it wants to protect you. It knows that baggage from the past can and will be brought in your current life, including how you are perceived.

Your inner critic doesn't know the right way to go about help-ing you. Your inner critic (you) wants you to speak well, wants your marriage and business to work. It does not want you to let pasts hurt ruin you in the present moment or in the future.

You can think of your inner critic like a fire and brimstone preacher like televangelist Joel Osteen's father was. Fire and brim-stone preachers mission is to scare the hell out of religious people who are sometimes mockingly called Bible-toting Christians.

These preachers tell their parishioners that if they don't live righteously and according to the Bible they are going to hell. Of course they don't want anyone to go to hell so they make hell scary.

You are going to burn alive in the fiery pit like a barbecue.

The preacher does not know for sure what hell looks like but he paints a picture so vivid that one can almost picture skin melt-ing off the bone.

Your inner critic is like the yapping preacher who believes if he gives you no mercy he can scare you into doing better. It's the same tactic used by an overly concerned parent or teacher who wants you to do well in school. Here you are thinking your parent or your teacher is a bitch, when all they wanted you to do is improve your grades.

Bad grades are coming. You aren't going to graduate.

Your inner critic shows at the most vulnerable moments and it activates a sign of trouble.

Fire is coming. Failure is coming. Your Marriage isn't succeeding because you can't communicate and none of your relationships will succeed either. Your business is not succeeding because your voice does not sound nice when you make sales calls.

Your inner critic shows up for big and small things too. He'll show up before, during and after a date. He's got bad news before you go on a date.

She won't show up.

He's got bad news during the date.

She's not really feeling me and doesn't think I'm interesting.

He's got bad news after the date.

She won't go on a second date with you.

The inner critic is all over you like Conor McGregor is on his opponent. Bang. Bang. Boom. Smack.

HOW TO DEAL WITH A NASTY INNER CRITIC?

Your inner critics loves "You on You" action. Which means you are attacking you. I hope you got that joke, if not, let me clear it up. Your inner critic is you. "You on You" action. Oh, never mind.

There are several ways to deal with a nasty inner critic:

- Pep Talk
- Mindfulness
- Edit self-talk
- Fight

PEP TALK

When your inner critic beats up on you it is necessary that you jump outside your head and evaluate the negative statements. You want to give yourself a pep talk to separate and evaluate fact from fiction, lies from truths, from exaggerations.

If it helps you can write down your pep talk (speech) or you can pretend you are a coach, coaching yourself. Put on your football cleats and coach the game already.

It might help you when thinking about the right things to say to yourself to first realize that you are not alone. There are millions of people on this planet with speech problems, failed marriages and businesses. Or dealing with whatever situation you are dealing with.

Your pep talk can begin with the reminder that you are not alone.

I am not alone, every guy (and woman for that matter) has an inner critic who is a hater.

Include a series of questions in your pep talk.

How did this guy or that one get over himself or overcome his painful early beginnings?

Remind yourself that even if they didn't overcome, that does not mean you can't.

I can overcome because I have more willpower and determination than the average guy. I'm not afraid to seek help.

My client received therapy for his speech problems and he became a much better speaker. He received counseling for his failed marriage and it helped him to realize that marriages fail, people aren't bad and sometimes they grow apart. He learned when people grow apart they sometimes say and do nasty things to one another. He also learned that it is possible to rebound and find love again after a failed marriage.

My client later reconnected with his business partner, no they didn't go into business together again, but they were able to talk things out and heal old wounds.

As a woman I believe in mantras: I can. I will. I did.

I suggest men use a MANtra too.

Chant over and over again, "It's not as bad as it seems. It's not as bad as it seems."

I know when your internal voice starts criticizing and lashing out at you it feels like you are under attack. It may feel as if everything is crashing all around you. Like somebody dropped a bomb.

Because our brain doesn't distinguish between imagination and reality the internal attacks are perceived by our mind as something real, a real and physical attack. Your brain generates an automatic emotional and physical response.

Even though it isn't really happening you start having symptoms like it is. Your heart beats faster. You breathe faster. Your muscles tighten. Your vision can become blurred and so forth.

Harvard trained physiologist Walter Cannon coined the phrase fight-or-flight (acute stress response), which is a reaction to how our body responds to real or imagined things. Because our brain doesn't distinguish between the two, imagined things feel real.

This is why men love action movies and why women are scared shitless by scary movies. Even though you know it's just a fake movie, it feels real.

You get the thrills without the punishment. A car crashes in the action movie and it's exciting even though it's not you and it's not real.

A character gets killed and you are terrified, but it's not you and it's not real.

The fight-or-flight goes back to our cave days in which such responses were needed to survive. In cave days if you weren't prepared for danger you risked losing your life.

Whether real or imagined our brains generate emotional and physical responses. For some the feelings are beyond intense.

- **Rapid Heart Beat and Breathing:** Your heart rate and respiration rates increase to provide the oxygen and energy the body needs to fuel a rapid response to what is either real or perceived danger.

- **Discolored skin:** When you become stressed blood will flow from the surface areas of the body to the muscles, brain, and other body parts. You may become pale or red in the face.

- **Dilated pupils:** The body prepares itself to become more alert, observant and aware of its surroundings and this can cause eyes to twitch or pupils to dilate.

- **Shaking or trembling.** When you are stressed or nervous your body may shake or tremble as it gets prepared for intense action.

This type of body responses can be embarrassing although the body is using immediate defense mechanisms.

Imagine how weird my client felt sitting in the cafeteria wanting to hang out with the other kids. He undoubtedly felt frightened. What if he gets noticed and one of the kids comes over to beat him up? I can imagine that he was feeling scared and also the insatiable desire of curiosity, of wanting to belong.

You can imagine his brain firing up the adrenaline and cortisol, which caused all types of symptoms like rapid heartbeat, sweating and or weird facial expressions. He probably looked like he was creepy when in reality he was scared shitless.

MINDFULNESS

Start your day with a few minutes of mindfulness which will bring you greater clarity, peace of mind and less harassment from your inner critic. *Psychology Today* defines mindfulness as a state of active, open attention on the present.

When you're mindful you carefully observe your thoughts and feelings without judging them good or bad. Instead of letting your life pass you by mindfulness means living in the moment and awakening to your current experience, rather than dwelling on the past or thinking about the future.

Mindfulness may sound a bit "new agey" to some and like one of those words you want to skip over but there's a reason why mind-fulness, which when you boil it down to its essence, simply means being present in the moment, is such a powerful state of being. Whatever you call it recognize its power against your inner critic.

Not being mindful in regards to my client's situation previ-ously meant spending a great portion of his day focusing on past problems. He's no longer in school, in the bad marriage, or in the bad business. He's free from it all. Free to spend that time and energy on the present moment.

If you are out on a date or at a social gathering be tuned into the present moment. What is she wearing? How does she smell? What are her needs? What are your needs?

Your focus shouldn't be on your date last week that didn't go well, or the business deal or job opportunity that didn't come through. That's negative energy that you don't need in your present moment.

EDIT SELF

Words are very powerful. They deserve a great deal of respect which is why you must edit your self-talk before your date.

When you edit yourself you delete, cross or scratch out the negativity.

This date, like the last date and the one before that is not going to work out. Edit that negative statement.

This date could potentially be the best date I'd ever had. You've edited out the negativity and you are going on this next date starting off with the correct mindset.

Embracing positive thoughts enables you to grow as a person and become self-aware. Instead of pushing away or ignoring your inner critic, invite your inner critic in and have a conversation. Your inner critic spews negativity, you correct him with positive talk as you become more aware of his tactics.

FIGHT BACK

It's all about the survival of the fittest. I just love putting my readers in real life scenarios. It goes like this:

You have a date set up with an attractive woman and you are very much looking forward to it.

Unfortunately, you've let your inner critic get in your head (despite the pep talk and self-editing) and tell you that this woman really doesn't want to go on a date with you.

To make matters worse, on your way to the date you get in your car and discover that you have a flat tire. Help is on the way but still you are going to be late for the date.

Your inner critic has already been bouncing in your head telling you that this woman does not want to go on a date with you.

Knowing that you are going to be late for the date your inner critic doubles down on you and reinforces that your date doesn't really like you and if you are late it will give her an excuse to bail and to cancel future dates. All is lost.

Ask yourself, if the woman was not interested in you why would she agree to a date? If you are late she might eventually leave but does that mean she won't go on another date with you?

Oh, I know she won't go on another date with you because she doesn't like you. Then why in the hell would she be going out with you? I get it, she's taking pity on you? You see how this could turn into a never-ending cycle of lunacy like an old faulty washing machine?

You must exit your head and give yourself a pep talk, edit your negative self-talk, think reasonably and if all else fails fight back. Start with asking yourself questions and giving reasonable answers.

Do you think a woman has time to go on pity dates?

What reason would this woman have to pity you? You are an above average looking guy and you are successful. She may not know you well but what she does know she likes and has agreed to a date.

If a woman leaves before you arrive and then later does not return your call because you had an honest reason for being late on the first date, is that more about her than you?

Does it mean that she really doesn't like you? Or is she going off a past experience with a prior boyfriend who was always late and now she gives no mercy to guys being late?

If she does cancel the date you can't possibly know the reason if she does not tell you. If she doesn't tell you then remember the Henry Ford quote, with a twist to it. If you think it's correct it is.

If you don't know the reason she canceled shouldn't you first ask why? If you tried to follow-up with her and she didn't return your phone call that still does not mean she's not interested in you. Maybe she backed away from you because the moment she laid her eyes on you she was smitten.

Why can't that be true? Why can't you tell yourself something favorable? This is about fighting back and neutralizing the power of your inner critic.

The way that an inner critic is able to take full advantage of you and catch you at your most vulnerable moment is when you don't have a comeback and or if you haven't fully prepared for a situation.

I've covered the need to be prepared for dating or going on a date in other parts of this book. It's important to bring up the subject again in this chapter because the inner critic loves to bother you when you are most vulnerable and when you haven't dotted your I's and crossed your T's. When you've forgotten your man kit.

Going on a date for some men makes them feel nervous like going to a job interview or giving a speech. But in that situation you've been coached on what to wear, how to answer questions, how to speak, and the best body language to use, etc.

In other words, you have to be prepared for best case and worst course scenarios. You have to carry and utilize your male survival bag.

CRAFT YOUR STORY

Your inner critic is a liar and a damn good storyteller. You are good at what you do. If you can't befriend or reason with your inner critic you have to beat his ass. You have to tell yourself the story you need to hear. He sets the clarion call and you set it off by telling yourself a more powerful story.

Tell yourself a story that sings your praises. Crafting your story is bringing all the elements together: The pep-talk. The mindfulness. The editing out negativity and when all us fails, the fighting spirit.

If you tell yourself in a powerful way that you can overcome challenges, you can. If you tell yourself you can get the girl, you can. If you believe you can have women at your feet and always trying to pick you up, you can. If you believe you can marry the woman of your dreams, you can.

My client, remember him, with the speech impediment, the so-called weird guy? I matched him up with the woman of his dreams and he has a very successful business and an amazing life.

None of the things that my client went through defined him, or held him back. He overcame each and every single one of them, and if he can, you can too!

KEY TAKEAWAYS

Your early life experiences shape the powerfulness of your inner critic according to psychologist Robert Firestone. Early hurts and pains will follow you and if not dealt with will cause pain for as long as you let it without doing something about it.

Your inner critic is nasty as a way to protect you. He is like those fire and brimstone preachers, they want to protect you from going to hell so they try to scare the crap out of you. It's the same tactic some parents and teachers use.

There are many ways to deal with an inner critic. It first starts with jumping out of your head and into reality. You can give yourself a pep talk, as if you were a coach, coaching yourself.

Remind yourself there are lots of people who are going through what you are going through or went through and many overcame. Even if some didn't overcome that does not mean you can't.

The fight-or-flight response means we react emotionally and our body reacts physically to real or imagined danger. If you watch a movie that has danger and or scary scenes your brain cannot distinguish between what's real and what is not.

Mindfulness boils down to being present in the moment and is mentioned throughout this book because it works. It may come across as some new age way of thinking but in layman's terms it simply means to not focus on your negative past, something you can't change or an unpredictable future, something you can't forecast. Instead, it means to check into the current space you occupy.

Focus entirely on the very moment that you are in. If you are on a date with a woman focus on how good she looks and smells.

Edit self-talk. This is self-correction. Instead of talking and thinking negatively, think positive. Don't let your inner critic craft your story. That's letting the liar talk bad about you.

My client overcame BIG time and you can too.

CHAPTER 14

QUALIFY, THEN MESMERIZE – THE MESMERIZE EFFECT

The eyes are the windows of the soul

- Thomas Phaer

THIS CHAPTER CONTAINS a special treat for you.

I've talked a lot about ways you can attract a woman and how to do it. I've discussed at length what your approach should be if you want to unlock her legs or her heart.

If you're more interested in unlocking a lovely woman's heart, then it's important you qualify her to meet your requirements. You do this by going through a qualification assessment.

The most important part of this assessment is to find the answer to this simple question: *"Does she qualify?"* In other words, is she good enough for you? I'm about to explain carefully why you shouldn't take this qualification for granted.

Suppose you meet a woman. Everything comes together for the both of you after you meet, not unlike a game of Escape. You do remember the Escape adventure game that I mentioned in the *Small Talk* chapter of this book, yes? The game is inspired by the 'escape - the - room' concept, in which all the clues you gather must come together to accomplish the mission to break free.

In the world of singlehood, where you mingle with, date and attract women, everything you discovered and learned in this book must come together so you captivate the woman of your dreams, whether in a romantic, monogamous relationship, or in bed.

You want to connect the dots and put together the facts to determine if she's the right one for you. If she doesn't meet your expectations on several of the qualifications and your gut feeling about her is not positive, you might want to go with your gut feeling. Your man's intuition.

Let me tell you something: if you're able to improve on just a fraction of the different aspects of verbal and nonverbal communication laid out in this book, including (but not limited to) small talk, body language, eye contact, a good sense of humor, being in the moment, being an active listener, and being authentic, I can all but guarantee that you will meet and form memorable relationships with women on a frequent basis.

If your primary objective is to improve your charisma to the extent that you're attracting more women more often, then you'll find the key to unlocking your dreams in these pages.

You now know what a man needs to do to charm and date women in this day and age and how he needs to go about doing it. In this chapter you are going to learn the techniques you can apply to your personal life to take your game one step further. Before you do that however, you will want to take the time to qualify her. Don't pull out the stops to mesmerize her just yet. Memorize: qualify, then mesmerize.

Assessing her character will enable you to get to the best part of the qualification process. This is the part where you ask yourself one of the most vital questions a single man who wants to date can possibly ask himself: "What's in it for me?" (WIIFM?).

This isn't about being selfish and instead it's about relationships having two halves. What you need and what she needs.

Now that you've gone over and above to learn how to impress a woman and bring out the better part of your authentic self, it's time for *her* to impress you. Your thoughts and feelings do in fact matter in the dating process.

The buck does not stop with her simply showing an interest in you; that's insufficient and you deserve better. After you've built a rapport with her (whether it's after one date or after a series of dates and other meetings), it's high time for her to show *you* why she's a great catch.

In the spirit of equality and reciprocity, she must impress you in the same way you impressed *her*. If she winds up impressing you even more, well... even better because after all charisma and dating has two halves.

You may have assumed that attracting a woman in and of itself is enough and it may be if you are looking for a specific outcome that doesn't require that much effort, but if you're looking to shift from sex to stability, you'll have to revisit that assumption.

When you begin utilizing the different strategies I've shared with you in this book, the act of attracting and dating women in itself is bound to become easier for you. I'm not going to say women will be throwing themselves at you, but some will certainly go out of their way to get your attention.

If you're yearning for something with a little more longevity and commitment to it however, you owe it to yourself to qualify her.

Having said that, let me avoid doubt by saying this: do not, I repeat, do not, make her feel as though she is being interviewed for a job position, or that she is an unwilling participant in a competition where she has to qualify.

Or worst, don't dare interrogate her. Instead, use a casual yet intentional approach to determine if she's the one with whom you want to take it to the next level or dating phase, try asking open-ended questions like:

- *"What would you consider your best trait?"*

- *"What makes you stand out from or more special than other women?"*

- *"What are at least two things about you that make you different and a one-of-a-kind?"*

This is light (yet serious) small talk that does not come across as an interrogation. Phrase the questions above in a manner which suits you best so that they feel natural to you, because the worst thing you can do when trying to qualify her is unqualify yourself by sounding ridiculous.

One qualifier of yours she's already passed is that you find her physically attractive, which in almost all instances is the first thing men use as a qualifier. You men have animalistic instincts when it comes to what you consider to be visually appealing and I mean that in a good way.

We all know women who are beautiful; some are strikingly so. Let's use a different term here though such as "enthralling", women who you find great difficulty taking your eyes off of.

Note that this and other qualifiers can make a woman more or less attractive in your eyes once you have begun asking her questions.

The answers she gives you to your qualifying questions are a test of her mental attractiveness which exhibits itself primarily as confidence. Her responses are in themselves qualifiers. Don't just judge her words, judge her body language and inflection of her words as she delivers them.

If you choose to follow Dr. Albert Mehrabian's study, here is how you assign her points:

- *7% goes to the importance of the words she uses.*
- *Tone of voice gets 38%.*
- *Face and body language get a whopping 55%.*

Pay close attention to her body language and words used when she answers you. Remember: when words and body language don't match, body language prevails.

Does she maintain eye contact, or are her eyes wandering? Does she appear excitedly nervous, aloof, or like she's flat-out lying?

Does her posture exude confidence, or disinterest? Confidence as observed through a woman's body language may also involve taking up space. She may be wearing a skirt though so forgive her if she does not sit with her legs apart. Instead her confidence will be revealed by the way her legs are crossed and where her arms are positioned.

If she's displaying confident body language she may place her arm on the armrest of the chair she is sitting on or standing near (provided that there is an armrest to rest on, of course). She may also extend her forearms along the length of the chair's armrest which indicates a state of relaxation.

If she is confident, comfortable and certain, she won't be doing any fidgeting with her arms or hands. She won't slouch; a confident, truthful woman will keep her shoulders upright and her back straight. She will never put her hands on her stomach.

As she gazes directly into your eyes she will lower her tone, her voice, and may raise both ever so gently to emphasize a point in the answers she gives to your questions.

Confidence is virtually irresistible and you might be tempted to swipe your tongue across her glossed lips.

Women find a confident man sexy and the reverse holds true as well. In relationships, as with anything else in life, a confident person is an indicator of her solid qualifications. Why is this, you ask? Well, let's face it: relationships, also as with anything else in life, will present their own challenges and obstacles. Interpersonal issues are also bound to arise, such as jealousy, envy and emotional unfulfillment.

Beautiful women are a dime a dozen, high-quality beautiful women, not so much. Your improved charisma and charm will cause all types of women to flock to you like a magnet, even when you're not actively trying to pursue them. A woman who is self-assured will not suspect, complain or worry about you lusting after other women and she won't even consider that you are cheating.

A self-assured woman will trust in her own ability to give you her undivided attention, make you happy and keep you sexually satisfied. She will be and remain faithful to you, even if you were not faithful yourself. Her confidence in herself as a woman will recognize that what caused you to cheat had nothing to do with her as a person, or with anything she did or failed to do as your partner.

(Please do not think that I am giving you permission to cheat.) What I am saying is that a self-assured woman will not blame herself for a mistake you made. She realizes that your mistakes are precisely that, yours, and you must own them.

The conversation you have with her should also be an exploration of her mental intelligence and more importantly, her emotional intelligence. Her mental intelligence speaks to her education or academic level. She doesn't need a Ph.D. but can she read and write?

Is she able to perform simple mathematic calculations without the aid of using her fingers or her phone? Can she read for longer than a few minutes? What's crucial however is her emotional intelligence. This is what will set her apart from other women.

Emotional intelligence is the ability to control and express one's emotions. Even though it is common knowledge that women are more emotional than men, still she must have the ability to self-regulate what she feels and what she says or does based on those feelings.

Emotional intelligence is knowing the right thing to say at the right time and in the right situations. This is key. Think about it - you've probably been with a woman who constantly misspeaks and comes off as an airhead, or you know someone who has. It is a disaster waiting to happen, the likes of which you should avoid.

I have a friend who, bless her heart, only *sounds* like she is articulate or knows what she's talking about. She's attractive and always dresses to impress, but most of the time she reveals too much about herself and she has no filter. She just doesn't know how to strike a balance between not disclosing enough and disclosing too much. Ideally, conversations should be equal, with each person revealing a comparable amount of information about themselves.

Intelligence is easy to come by. All you need to fit society's definition of "intelligent" is to get an education, be an avid learner or reader, maybe achieve a high grade on some standardized test. Emotional intelligence is significantly harder to come by, chiefly because it can't be taught. A woman who lacks emotional intelligence lacks self-awareness, which in turn may lead to a lack of social skills. That's a problem.

If a woman lacks emotional intelligence her looks won't matter in the long-term; eventually, having sex with her (together with the physical attractiveness which makes it enjoyable) will get old and you'll get bored.

Maturity is another qualifier. Women mature faster than men, generally speaking, but that's not a hard and fast rule. If she's emotionally needy or clingy be prepared to experience some immature behavior. What probably has attracted her to you is one of your power traits.

Don't think because this is your first date or first couple of dates that she won't display this behavior; the truth of a woman's insecurity or immaturity will always reveal itself, sometimes sooner than you realize or are ready for.

A successful man or one on his way to success loses interest if a woman tries to pull him in every direction. Setting your schedules, instructing you on how to dress, it can be overwhelming and a reason not to go any further with her.

Independence is a qualifier to consider. This need not include financial independence (unless you want it to). If she has a hobby, charity or interest, or if she has her own professional ambitions, this will prevent her from being bored and finding ways to interfere with your aspirations for success.

These qualifiers, together with the questions you may ask are a starting point and a solid reminder that women should meet your expectations too.

QUALIFIED? TIME TO MESMERIZE!

Now that the woman of your focus is qualified, it's time to mesmerize her. This chapter's title is such that you may have been tempted to read it first. The ability to mesmerize is so powerful, even the word "mesmerize" is a trap to lure you in.

Just know that you will need the full benefit of each chapter to really mesmerize her. If you came right to this chapter, be sure to go back and read the others first. It'll be worth it, I promise!

Pretend that you are an actor on a movie set in the beautiful resort town of Punta Cana. The stage is set and the town is bustling with activity. The only instructions you've been given by the director is to pick from one of the many attractive actresses on the set and mesmerize her.

That's it. You look at the director incredulously. She can't be serious, surely, she has more details to give? You frown because, well the director needs to give you some type of instructions on how to mesmerize one of these beauties.

The director ignores you. She's a bitch and a half. You look around the set nervously at the actresses standing before you. Each actress looks lovelier than the next. You hope that someone, anyone on the set will reveal what you are supposed to do. No one says a word or even gives you hints with their body language. The director frowns and yells, "Are you ready?"

That's it. Three words and less than three seconds, the director yells:

"READY... SET... ACTION!"

This is your big opportunity. You walk up to one of the beautiful actresses with as much determination as you can muster. You're taking big strides. Your back is fully erect. Your shoulders are standing tall. You are staring one of the actresses directly into her eyes. You approach the actress and lean over to plant a kiss on her cheek.

The director screams, "Cut!" She then yells, "That's not how you mesmerize a lady. I don't have time for this. Get this amateur out of here!"

You are puzzled. Your acting career is over before it began and you don't know why. But screw the acting career, all you really want to know is how do you get a woman's undivided attention so that she cannot think of anything else but you? You want to mesmerize her in such a way that she'll liken it to being hypnotized.

You may have looked into a woman's eyes before and felt mesmerized. This may mean that you were captivated by her beauty to the extent that you felt hypnotized for a short period of time.

Certainly, you've heard a woman say, "I looked into his eyes, and I was mesmerized." What that means is that she felt euphoric, weak, vulnerable or powerless, but in a good way.

The truth about mesmerizing a woman is that no two women can be mesmerized in exactly the same way (just like no two women will qualify for you in exactly the same way). There are also a variety of ways to seduce a woman.

You should recall I use an informal screening process that is like a group of friends sharing drinks and laughs to evaluate women for our matchmaking database. It is through the screening process and my collection of what I learned by conversing with hundreds (if not thousands) of woman that I discovered the variety of ways in which you can mesmerize a woman.

Different women have different opinions on what set of actions and words demonstrate charisma. In a similar vein, they can be mesmerized in different ways. Melissa won't be mesmerized in the same way as Claire, Emily or Mia.

Here are several ways to mesmerize her. Bear in mind that some things are more appropriate to do only when you are dating.

THE FIRST MEETING: WHAT TO DO

Body language. If you are at a social gathering and an attractive woman from across the room catches your eye and you catch her eye, you want to send a signal to her which she will easily recognize as seduction, even in a crowd. You can do this with a head tilt. When you tilt (cock) your head, it subconsciously signals to a woman that you are interested and that you're daring her to make the first move.

You are showing that you are approachable. You are showing that you desire her. The tilt of your head is a special invitation for her to come closer.

If you know you look good meaning you are well-groomed and nicely dressed. You may even try penetrating her with your eyes, and if you are feeling especially good rub your tongue against your bottom lip.

Woman have a special intuition that lets them know when you are trying to seduce her.

Be warned though, not every man can pull this off. This takes practice because you certainly don't want to come across as a creep. If you come across as creepy, someone she may need to report, then you have it all wrong.

If you get it right you will be able to lure her over with your body talk and then lube her up with the sexy flirty small talk covered in the chapter so named. Small talk, the big social lubricant.

Ask anyone who's been somewhere waiting for her friend and feeling nervous. There's nothing more seductive and calming than having a cute guy making eyes at her.

GETTING TO KNOW HER WITH A SENSE OF TOUCH

Women especially enjoy the touch of a man's hands. A man's touch can be nurturing. Provided that she consents, she is likely to enjoy the stroking of a man's hands over her clothing or sensitive areas that make her nerves tingle. A massage is one of the most sensual forms of touching possible. It's the ultimate way to mesmerize.

You don't have to be a masseuse to give her a massage that will set her on fire and make her moist. How deep you go about giving the massage will depend on how well you know the woman and her giving consent. The key to a good massage is the setting. You want the settings sound, look (& feel), and smell to be fantastic.

This means dim the lights or close the curtains. Play some music or use an app with relaxing sounds. You want to give the massage in a comfortable setting. Next you want to be sure the atmosphere smells amazing. Find out beforehand what her favorite candle or oil scent is.

Before you begin, brush your lips against her neck and chin. This is what the actor did wrong in the hypothetical scene above instead of going in for the kiss. He needed to tease her first. The skin on the neck is thin and melts to the touch of lips or hands.

Next, think of your hands like human instruments and play around on her back like you would any other part of her body. Apply pressure, squeeze, cup, - first gently then a little harder, harder, faster, faster, slower. Be sure not to cause pain, unless she tells you otherwise. Find the knots and smooth them out.

Other places to touch her to make her squirm are:

Her inner wrist (tap, tap, gently)

Her hair (sweep it away from her face)

Her waist (tap, tap and squeeze gently)

Her feet (women enjoy a good foot massage)

The back of her neck (gently run your fingers from her neck to her back)

The center and small of her back (massage and big squeezes)

The warmth of your body against her chest will cause her brain to release a surge of oxytocin known as the 'cuddle hormone' to get her in a feisty mood.

THE FIRST MEETING: THE SCENTS AND FRAGRANCES

Have you ever been in the company of a woman who smelled absolutely delightful, like a sweet blend of soft fragrances or a delicious combination of exotic fruit? Have you ever been so turned on by her fragrance that you could practically taste your longing for her? That's the power of the sense of smell.

When a woman is in the company of a man who smells fresh and clean, it makes her instantly attracted to him. Don't be that guy who doesn't shower and wears dingy clothes in public, or who attempts to mask his body odor with cologne. That's nasty! Be fresh at all times.

You want to know what scents attract a woman? Each woman has their own preference but here are scents known to turn women on:

Musk: Smells of male pheromones and drives women crazy. You can't go wrong with a cologne that has musk as the main ingredient.

Peppermint: Boosts energy and puts those who can smell it in a better mood. Peppermint helps you stay awake and energized so that a woman can tune into you, and you alone. Peppermint scent also opens her up.

Vanilla: Subtle, sweet and welcoming. This scent increases sexual stimulation in women and men alike.

Patchouli: This earthy aroma makes women horny. It awakens sexual energy with its strong, slightly sweet smell.

Jasmine: The aromatic varieties of jasmine are known for their intense, sharp and sweet fragrance. It is capable of bringing calm to frayed nerves and a stressed spirit.

Ylang Ylang: This activates the romantic side of you. It has a relaxing, floral and fresh scent which varies greatly due to differences in commercial grades. It is not common for a mean to wear a floral scent, but he can spray it or use incense.

Women are huge fans of scents. I know of more than one single lady who goes in the cologne departments of stores or malls and spray men's colognes in the air or on themselves whenever they are feeling lonely.

Romance books with a ripped, handsome guy on the cover, fly off the shelves. Those books would lead you to believe that all a man had to do to seduce a woman is to look good. Inside the book you learn that not only must he look good, he must be filthy rich.

That's it, those two things are all that are needed to seduce. Really?

In real life it doesn't work that way. In the real world it takes more than looks and money to captivate a high-quality woman. Mesmerizing a woman is not totally about how you look or what you have, it's more about how you make her feel, keeping in mind that no two women will want it the same way.

Make her feel good and you are well on your way to having what has been called the mesmerizing effect!

KEY TAKEAWAYS

Qualify her by assessing her character. Not as if she's in a job interview or an interrogation. Instead your questions should be casual and informal.

Assign her points (this is for your purposes only), using if you like Dr. Mehrabian's percentages. What is her body language communicating with you? Is it a language of confidence and other attractive traits?

What is her conversation like? Does she have a filter? Does she tell too much about her business or other's business?

What is her level of education and most importantly is she emotionally intelligent? Is she mature and independent?

The actor in the pretend movie scene screwed up royally, don't let that be you.

To send seductive signals to a woman you want to tilt/cock your head, penetrate her with your eyes, rub your tongue against the bottom of your lip. Proceed with caution, you don't want to come across as a creep. Read her body language to gauge if she's interested.

Women especially enjoy a man's touch and will appreciate a good massage. The key to a good massage is setting.

You set a mesmerizing setting with sound, look (& feel), and smell good scents.

Aside from a massage there are other places to touch a woman that will cause her to melt: Inner wrist, hair, waist, feet, neck and back.

There are known fragrances that turn women on. Musk, Peppermint, Vanilla, Patchouli, Jasmine, Ylang Ylang.

CONCLUSION

WELL HONEY, WE'VE come to an end, which means a new beginning for you. I have to let you go for now. We began this journey with me asking you to imagine that you're waltzing off a private jet into the soft island-ish feel, resort town of Punta Cana with the blue sky, the white sand beaches that stretch as far as the eye can see and the crystal clear waters where a bevy of beauties relax along the shore.

I asked you to come along as I acted as your personal social interaction coach to show you ways to turn on your charisma and spice up your dating life. I was upfront with you that you might not have always liked what I had to say, but I would never steer you in the wrong direction. Did I lie?

I told you that whatever you desire, a one-night stand or an everlasting relationship - can be yours as long as you are willing to keep an open mind and oh yeah, apply the self-improvement advice shared.

I'm going to leave you with some parting advice. It's the absolute best advice pulled from the book and a reminder that with a little work you can completely redesign your love life and make it exactly what you desire.

CHARISMA NEEDS CULTIVATING

The word charisma means different things to different people. It's not an unobtainable thing like the man who married his cousin would have us to believe. It's not innate and at best it's 50-50.

Some are born with some charisma. Some possess power traits that give them a football-field-wide advantage. These traits are power, wealth, fame, looks and, oh screw them.

The Good News: If you weren't born with a charismatic bone in your body or you don't have the power traits that give you a boost, you can grow some. You see, charisma isn't like fine wine or cheese and age isn't the only thing that can make it better - it gets better with practice.

It must be cultivated, nurtured and not taken for granted. You reap what you sow.

As you move through different phases of your life things will change. Yep, power, wealth, looks, fame sometimes fade away. And with age, your charming personality that you've cultivated might come with a bit of crankiness. When stuff changes your confidence can take a hit.

That's why whatever you do, never stop cultivating and seeking to be a better man. Even if at some point you leave the dating game and you get the girl of your dreams to meet you down the aisle, you better know that what it took to get her is what it takes to keep her.

BE COOL

You are going to make mistakes in dating. Sometimes it's going to be your fault and sometimes it's going to be her fault. There's rarely anything you can do or say that you can't recover from and if that is ever the case it's simply not meant to be.

You can meet an attractive woman someplace and offer to buy her a drink. She's with a friend so you also offer to buy her friend a drink because you think it's the gentlemanly thing to do, and it is. For whatever reason, this causes jealousy in this woman and she leaves you, her drink and her friend at the bar.

You kick yourself thinking what you did wrong. You didn't do anything wrong - it was just not meant to be.

You could have been dating a girl for a while and things have been going great, or so you think. Then one day she suddenly stops returning your phone calls and you beat yourself up wondering what did you do wrong? You did nothing wrong - it just wasn't meant to be.

Worst-case scenario it was something you did – it was your fault. In that case, just be cool and let it roll off your sleeve. The worst thing you can do is beg and stalk her. That will only make it worse and is she really worth all of that?

CHARISMA MINDSET

Bingo. The charisma mindset is everything. My favorite quote in this book of the many shared is by Henry Ford, "Whether you think you can, or you think you can't - you're right."

Stop right now and think of one of the hardest things you've ever set out to accomplish in your life.

Maybe it was graduating from college, losing a lot of weight, or learning to fly a plane. Whatever it was it took two things: practice and the right mindset. If you believed you could, you did.

Renowned psychologist Carol Dweck is a leading researcher in the field of motivation. She researches and writes about fixed vs. growth mindset. Someone with a fixed mindset will read this book and think of every excuse in the world why they can't exude charisma or have an exciting dating life. They might appreciate the advice I've shared although they won't believe it will work for them. They have a fixed mindset.

On the other hand, someone with a growth mindset will congratulate themselves for taking another step to improve their dating life by reading this book. They will know that after this book they must take ACTION and put what they learned to work. Get to work.

I shared the example of my client with the speech impediment. What I didn't share with you was the intense struggle he went through to overcome it. He went through hell. He went to hell and back but because he always knew he could overcome it, he did. I'm so proud of him. His growth mindset paid off and yours can too.

If ever your mind wanders into the lack-of-confidence arena, I want you to throw on Conor McGregor's boxing gloves. If you hate him then throw on the gloves of someone you admire. Stand on their shoulders. Morph into their way of thinking and fight your way to victory.

Invite your inner critic in; after all, the inner critic is there to protect you. He just goes about it the wrong way. He's like the preacher, the parent, or the teacher – who wants the best for you but has a terrible way of showing it.

You have to jump out of your head and into reality. Your inner critic is on some BS. He will pump you full of lies if you let him. He's good at messing with your head. You could be everything and a bag of chips but it's the one thing you lack that your inner critic attacks. Fight back with a pep talk and by connecting yourself with your congratulators.

THE PERCENTAGES

Dr. Albert Mehrabian's famous study attributes a whopping 93% of communication to words not spoken.

The breakdown:

7% relates to the importance of the words used

38% refers to voice tone and inflection

55% refers to the importance of face and body language

Here's some great news. The only percentage you have to remember is 7%. Not because it relates to words used but because if you can make a 7% improvement in yourself overall, you would be ahead of and far better than those who read this book then put it down and take no action. Take no action, get no action.

If you picked just one thing from each chapter to do, you'd get far ahead in the dating and charisma school of life.

Remember that verbal and nonverbal communication must play nicely together.

You don't only want to be skilled at saying all the right things and then your body language is telling a different story, because if body language and words don't match up, she'll believe your body language.

AUTHENTICITY

Every move you make and every action you take should stem from your authentic self - a place from which you build upon the strengths you already possess so you can enjoy better social interactions and improve your social presence.

You can't be someone you are not. You don't want to completely change "you", because believe it or not there is lots to like about you. You might not have been fully aware of that when you started reading this book but I have never worked with a client that didn't have any likable qualities.

There's an exercise that I have clients do where I ask them to take out a sheet of paper and list the qualities they have and then list the qualities they believe a woman wants in a man. They are always pleasantly surprised that they possess many of the qualities.

You'll recall that televangelist Joel Osteen after first taking over his father's church tried to imitate his father's fiery preaching style. Although his style was quite the opposite, being light-hearted and laid back, when he got started with the church he copied his father's style. He was worried that if he showed his authentic self the church would go from 5000 members to no members and close its doors.

Instead of the church decreasing in size, when he switched preaching styles the church grew from 5,000 to 25,000 members with millions of more supporters around the world. The reason the 5,000 members didn't leave and thousands more joined is because having charisma (or being likable) is in the eye of the beholder. If you like a lemon pie that does not mean you can't also like apple pie and maybe you'll even like it better.

Who are you? Go ahead and craft your story. Your story should start out with who you are and what your life is today. You can also include in the story how you envision your dating life in the future.

It's OK to aim high with relationship goals. It's called faking it until you make it. However, this is not about being fake or putting on a façade because remember, there are enough flaky people in the world already.

Though this does not mean that you can't write a fantastic story about you! You can write your story on paper or speak it into your phone and if you need a reminder on how to tell a good story, go back and read the *Charisma Holistic* chapter.

Trust me when I tell you that an exciting dating life is waiting for you, one filled with lots of options and exciting times.

You should know however that as you grow and mature (which has nothing to do with age, but a mentality), you'll probably get tired of so many girls coming in and out of your life. There will come a time when you'll want to, as the cowboys say, "Hang up your spurs and settle down." Will you be ready?

Human beings are flawed. Women are flawed, men are flawed and that's how the world is. Being flawed is not the same thing as not having your act together. You don't want a woman with a bunch of issues and vice versa. You want major issues resolved like unresolved mommy or daddy issues, past relationship drama etc. This is key because a man with a messy life will run a high-quality woman away.

Finally, and this is important, looks are important, it's understandable that you want an attractive woman on your arm, but I don't care if:

She's as beautiful as a sculpted goddess made from chocolate

It looks like rose petals fell from her ass when she walks by

She's a cutie and a beauty with the most amazing booty

Her looks will fade and you can either trade her in, or you can do the right thing and find someone who looks good both on the inside and out. If she's not a friend when her looks go, so might you.

This is in no way to suggest that you shouldn't find someone who you don't find attractive, but make sure she has other qualities too. Cute girls are a dime a dozen; high-quality women, not so much.

If you decide to play around in the dating app arena or take lessons from a love guru, there are a couple of things that I do not want you to forget. First, dating apps make people less social and no matter how many hot girls you find by swiping apps, nothing replaces the real thing. It's why digital toys also only take a woman so far.

Chances are you are not going to meet a high-quality woman on a dating app. The real high-quality women, if they do use an app, get swept up fast. If you spend too much time in the digital world your communication skills will suffer.

There is no replacement for real-life communication and effective communications skills. Plus, too much time in the digital world makes you less charitable and less likely to volunteer, qualities women find irresistible.

IS SHE QUALIFIED?

This entire book has been about things you can do to get her. But what about you? You matter too. Here I am turning you into this stud of a man, making you everything she ever wanted, but that won't matter if she's not the right one.

You want to qualify her. You don't want to spend all of your time and money on someone who is not the right one. A lady with her own deep-rooted issues is not the one.

You want to get to the heart of who she is, especially before things get serious. It's usually the case that men are the heartbreakers, but make no mistake about it - a well-qualified woman can break your heart too and the interesting thing is, it might not even be about you.

It could be that she has some unresolved issues that she was able to keep from you in the beginning. Just when you get ready to put a ring on it, Crazy Cathy, her alter ego comes from out of nowhere. She's super jealous and just because you take a look at an attractive woman, she assumes you are sleeping with her and she wants to slit your tires.

It could be that she's not independent. You may be an ambitious and/or powerful man which means you have to spend time handling your business affairs. You can't do that if she's always clinging to you, always jealous and always dealing with issues.

You won't run into these kinds of problems if you qualify her. If you qualify her you are less likely to get involved with a drama mama. The bottom line is, you deserve the best and should never settle for less in a long-term relationship.

Thank you and congratulations for finishing this book! You've taken a big first step. I hope this book was able to help you to find new confidence and understand how to build your natural power of charisma. Now you have to get out there and put these principles into practice and watch how drastically your charisma builds and your love life changes for the better.

If you enjoyed this book, then I'd like to ask you for a favor, would you be kind enough to leave an review for this book on Amazon? It would be greatly appreciated!

Finally, I'd love to hear your story. Tell me how you believe this book can help you, or if it has already helped you, I'd like to know. You can get in touch with me at: *www.angelaseitz.com*.

Here's to charisma, love, and dating happiness.

Warm Regards,

Angela

ABOUT THE AUTHOR

Angela Seitz is an author, speaker, certified charisma and social interaction coach and the Founder and CEO of 98 Palms, a luxury matchmaking vacation company located in the tropical paradise of Punta Cana, Dominican Republic.

With over ten years as one of the most unique matchmakers in the world, Angela has helped her private list of clients find love amidst their busy schedules. She is known by many as the "Love Concierge" for planning the most lavish and opulent customized dates for her matchmaking clients, ensuring the perfect atmosphere for falling in love.

Not only does Angela help busy gentlemen from all walks of life find romance, but she takes it one step further helping them to improve their charisma and social interaction skills so they can have much more success with women and in business.

www.ingramcontent.com/pod-product-compliance
Lightning Source LLC
Chambersburg PA
CBHW031506270326
41930CB00006B/274